TRANSCENDING WORRY

Philippians 4:1–13 considered at a time of Covid-19

John Bloor

Grosvenor House
Publishing Limited

This book is published by
Grosvenor House Publishing Ltd
Link House
140 The Broadway, Tolworth, Surrey, KT6 7HT.
www.grosvenorhousepublishing.co.uk

A CIP record for this book
is available from the British Library

ISBN 978-1-80381-538-1

Therefore, my brothers
you whom I love and long for,
my joy and crown,
that you should now stand firm in the Lord,
dear friends.
I plead with Euodia and I plead with Syntyche
to agree with each other in the Lord.
Yes and I ask you loyal yokefellow
help these women who have contended at my side
in the cause of the gospel,
along with Clement and the rest of my fellow-workers
whose names are in the Book of Life.
Rejoice in the Lord always. I will say it again, Rejoice.
Let your gentleness be evident to all.
The Lord is near.
Do not be anxious about anything
but in everything by prayer and petition
with thanksgiving
present your requests to God.
And the peace of God,
which transcends all understanding,
will guard your hearts
and your minds in Christ Jesus.
Finally, whatever is true,
whatever is noble,
whatever is right,
whatever is pure,
whatever is lovely,
whatever is admirable,

if anything is excellent or praiseworthy,
think about such things.
Whatever you have learned or received
or heard from me, or seen in me,
put it into practice.
And the God of peace will be with you.
I rejoice greatly in the Lord
that at last you have renewed your concern for me,
indeed you have been concerned,
but you had no opportunity to show it.
I am not saying this because I am in need,
for I have learned to be content whatever the circumstances.
I know what it is to be in need,
and I know what it is to have plenty.
I have learned the secret of being content,
in any and every situation,
whether well fed or hungry,
whether living in plenty or in want.
I can do everything through him who gives me strength.

Philippians 4:1–13.

This book is dedicated to the memory of
Dr Richard Bloor
February 1975 – July 2022

Also by John Bloor

The Impossible: Tracking Luke's Gospel (2010)

ACKNOWLEDGEMENTS

On John's behalf I would like to thank Saju Muthalaly friend, Vicar and now Bishop of Loughborough for all his support and encouragement throughout the years of writing this book. Your friendship meant so much to John. Thank you also Saju for your valuable contribution and personal experiences you were willing to share which so informed John's thinking and writing.

Thanks to St Mary's Island Church, Chatham, Kent for their love, care and prayers that carried John and I through a very difficult and painful time throughout the writing of this book and for their continuing support for me beyond. Matt Keeler, Lay Church Leader, thank you. Although you were unaware at the time, what you said that Sunday morning was the God inspiration behind this book. Particular appreciation to those members and friends from the church mentioned in this book who gave permission for John to write their stories and their experiences, which helped demonstrate and relate to particular points.

Thanks to my family Emma and Adam and Laura and Stuart and their families, and to Elaine and Brian, David and Maureen, who without their ongoing support, love and prayers, this book could not have made it to publication.

Thanks to our dear friends Julia and George who held us, prayed for us and encouraged John and I in the writing of this book.

Sally Bloor
February 2023

CONTENTS

THE ROAD TO EMMAUS

The supper at Emmaus by Rembrandt

Two people walking side by side and talking. They were not walking quickly. The seven miles from Jerusalem to Emmaus would take them all afternoon. A closer look would reveal that both were in great distress. The Roman authorities whilst being egged on by the Jewish leaders had taken Jesus of Nazareth who they had followed, and in whom they had placed their faith. They beat him half to death and finally they crucified him. The walkers had such high hopes that Jesus would lead Israel out of the crushing weight of foreign occupation. Now he was dead and they had witnessed it all. Their faith lay in tatters.

Unknown to them, another man was walking in the same direction out of Jerusalem. His walk was more energetic and so he soon overhauled the amblers. Now walking together, the two established that the stranger seemingly knew nothing about what had happened to Jesus. Perhaps that is why they poured it all out, their tears, frustration, anger, despair and worry. Their life ahead was an empty void with all the uncertainty that this bought with it.

The response to their outburst, when it had finally finished, may not have been quite what they expected. The stranger seemed oblivious to their pain. Instead, he berated them for their foolishness and then explained chapter and verse why this had happened. As he spoke, their hearts burned within them even to their uncomprehending minds. At last they reached Emmaus and the stranger said goodbye. Humbly they reached out to him.

Don't go.

It's getting late now

Stay with us.

Please

The stranger stopped and went with them to where they were staying. That evening something happened and their lives changed – forever. It is the same for anybody who asks this stranger to stay with them.

INTRODUCTION

*Therefore my brothers and sisters, you whom
I love and long for, my joy and crown*
Philippians 4:1

This is the opening verse of the most beautiful and often quoted passages in the Bible. I mused as I looked at it. It is rather like listening to the simple opening bars of a piece of music knowing that it is to about to develop into a desperately complicated fugue. So it is with Philippians 4:1–13. It opens with a love note from a man who longs to be with the people to whom he is writing. However, it develops into some mind-blowing claims. It is a passage familiar to both Christians and some who may not claim to be Christian at all.

"Philippians 4! I know that passage. Now let me see. It goes – 'Rejoice in the Lord always and again I say rejoice' It was read at my baptism." This was Elaine, my sister-in-law when she heard that I was writing a book on Philippians 4:1–13. Another person who I know well, recited the passage verbatim and she doesn't even go to church! I recall from my early Christian days, that this passage was quoted perhaps more than any other. A favourite quote was that final shout of triumph – "I can do everything through him who gives me strength" (Philippians 4:13). It was the thing to say to others especially when anyone felt defeated. If I dared to challenge this, the answer would come quickly back, "You've got to have faith, John. It's faith that will give you strength". I have often wondered whether I have that strength of faith. Can I do everything through him who gives me strength? Is this passage mind blowing or does it just go over our heads? This became very evident to me when I was in a zoomed prayer meeting with some lovely long-standing Christian friends.

"How are you getting along with the book?" they teased knowingly.

"Well I'm on my fourth re-write," I replied. They all laughed. I took my opportunity and good humouredly put them to the test.

"Look," I said, seeking to take no prisoners, "The passage says, 'Do not be anxious (or worried) about anything' (v5). Can you do that?" They looked dumb-faced and said nothing.

"OK" I went on. "What about, "Stand firm in the Lord" (v1). Are you doing that? They continued to look dumb faced but now with a few shaking heads.

Alright lastly – and this is a beauty! What about, "I have learned the secret of being content in any and every situation" (v12). Now they were open mouthed!

I started out thinking that somehow these three assertions flowed from one to the other and produced a happy result. I certainly thought that if I was not anxious, that I would have a better chance of standing firm. Then perhaps, pondering some more, if I am standing firm and not anxious, then I might be content in any and every situation. I was not sure. It might lead to a sporadic moment of contentment but not a contentment that would continue in all circumstances. The text also mentions that there is "a secret". If there is a secret then it is hidden, and if it is hidden, then I was going to have to dig to find out what it meant.

God prompted me to do just that and it took me on a journey of remembering and discovery. My journey turned out to be a very rocky road!

St Paul wrote this letter to the church at Philippi, Macedonia, when he was in the twilight of his years. He wrote it to a church he had founded and loved. It was written when he was in Rome, a prisoner probably under some form of house arrest while he waited for trial before the emperor to whom he had appealed. His lovely church at Philippi were worried about him so he wrote this letter now included in the New Testament known as "Philippians". The passage that I want to study comes toward the end of the letter. He wrote the letter to encourage the church, stressing the need of both faith and humility and to press forward to the goal of eternal life with a loving God. He wrote to instruct them to stand firm and not to be anxious or worried about anything He told them that he had found contentment in all circumstances. He knew that this challenge would not be easy so he blessed them with a blessing so often used in church services today – "the peace of the Lord which transcends all understanding will guard your hearts and your minds in Jesus Christ" (v7). So I put this together with worry and came up with the title to this book *Transcending Worry*. Looking beyond worry.

* * * *

A Christian friend said to me after she had read an early draft of this book, "John, can't I just worry a little bit?" We both laughed when we realised what she had said but her question held a great truth. We seem to want to hold on to familiarity even though it may cause much pain and suffering.

"Everybody worries, don't they?" asked a physiotherapist while putting me through some exercises.

I hesitated. "I don't know," I replied in all honesty. "Everybody that I know worries. I have heard the most seemingly self-confident people declare how much they worry but I cannot tell you for certain that everybody worries." My limitations came home to me. I know how much I worry. I know that many others worry to a greater or lesser extent. I am married to Sally who is a therapeutic counsellor. Especially through her, I realise that some people need professional help to adjust to experiences that have affected their anxious lives. Indeed, I have sought professional help myself. I am full of praise for those working in the fields of mental health.

Yet I do not think it's rocket science to conclude that most, if not all, people worry. I also think it safe to say that everyone wants some form of contentment. Possibly some find contentment sporadically but perhaps not contentment in any and every situation. I also think that people want to be able to stand firm where necessary and that many find this very difficult. Whilst having the earnest desire that this book might help worriers, I must stress that this is not a "fix-it" book. This is a "faith" book, faith in the God of Love who was born, lived, and walked in this world for some 30 plus years. God, in the world, is Jesus and it is in Jesus that we have our hope in transcending worry, standing firm and being content in any and every situation. All have this hope, a living hope, whatever our preconceived ideas may be if we ask Jesus to stay awhile. There is a secret out there, waiting to be found.

This is a book for ordinary people, about ordinary people written by an ordinary person about an extraordinary passage of writing inspired by a mighty and victorious God. God knows my ordinariness well as he knows us all. He knew that I would need careful handling. He knew that I would be reluctant to write this book because there was so much in the passage from Philippians that I did not understand. So I needed help and I got this from a friend. He is Varghese

Muthalaly Malayil Lukose which means George, the merchant, who lives on the hill whose father is Luke. Thankfully, his family had mercy on the rest of the world and he is known to us as Saju. My great friend Saju, erstwhile vicar of my church, now Bishop of Loughborough (as I write) will figure largely in these pages.

With the benefit of being able to look back, God's conception of this book began way before he nudged me in his inimitable way to write it. I can now see that God began planting *Transcending Worry* seeds when I went to Paris with Saju three years before I knew that I was to write it. This is what it is like being a servant of God.

CHAPTER ONE
TRANSCENDING WORRY

Do not be anxious about anything Philippians 4:6

On an overcast November morning, Saju and I were standing side by side at the western end of the Champs Élysées, in Paris. Saju, now my vicar and newly settled into leading the church, had appointed me to lay lead our daughter church. Then something completely unexpected happened.

"I want to go to Paris with you," said Saju to me one day after a staff meeting.

It is not often that I am taken completely by surprise but this was one of those moments. We were a very unlikely pair. Saju, then aged 38, stood tall, about 6'3", loved playing cricket and came from Kerala, South India while I, then aged 74, was an imposing 5'5" (and shrinking) and my youngest son was several years older than my travelling companion. Paris was easy to get to on Eurostar and I used to go two or three times every year. The trip proved significant both to our friendship and writing this book. Several Parisian sites that we visited feature in these pages interspersed with enjoying a glass of burgundy by the Seine. Much was deliberated over supper at the café next door to our hotel including the history of France from Napoleon Bonaparte, descending to a complete difference of opinion over the Virgin Mary, whilst settling back to the virtues of French wine.

On that November morning, we were looking up at what I consider to be the finest of all Paris monuments – the Arc de Triomphe. This huge edifice was the brainchild of the great Napoleon Bonaparte conceived in 1806 but not completed until 30 years later. It sits imposingly on top of a hill, on the Place de Charles de Gaulle, which forms the hub at the intersection of twelve streets radiating outwards, "comme une etoile" (like a star). Standing 50 metres tall and 45 metres wide, its elevations and arches are etched with 158 battles fought after the French revolution. At the base is the Tomb of the Unknown Warrior, where lies alone the remains of a French soldier who died in WW1 representing all who perished in that terrible conflict.

Anyone going to the Arc goes with two purposes. The first purpose is to look at the Arc from the outside and marvel at its size and grandeur and the second is to go inside and walk up the 280 steps to the roof. As we looked at the Arc from the outside, I pondered that, for all its magnificence, there is something very sad about this monument. The tragedy about the Arc is that it did not fulfil the purpose for which it was built. At the age of 37, Napoleon was at the height of his mental and physical faculties when he conceived the plan to build this enormous portal. Waterloo was still nine years away. His Grand Army looked impregnable. What could be better than a triumphant march through this huge and imposing construction. Yet it never took place. The nearest it got to happening is when

Napoleon's coffin was wheeled under the Arc in 1840 after his body was repatriated. Worst was to come. One hundred years later, Nazi Germany invaded France, took Paris and marched its triumphant army through the magnificent Arc. It was hardly what was envisaged by those who built it.

Inside the Arc, the steps are claustrophobic and crowded. As climbing continues, breathing becomes laboured. Stopping is not an option because of the people climbing behind. Then people start coming down, having become frightened or they just want to give up. Bodies meet and edge gingerly round each other as they negotiate the narrow winding stairs. But what a reward for those who persevere!

The view from the roof is the best view across Paris. Nowhere else matches it! That's odd because the Arc is nowhere near as high as the Eiffel Tower or the elevated position of Sacre Coeur in the Bohemian area of Montmartre. It stands at a height not far above rooftop level. Now rooftop level is very even across the centre of Paris. This is because in the 1860s, Napoleon's nephew, Napoleon III, decided to demolish and rebuild the city. This colossal undertaking will answer any question as to why all the buildings look the same with the same height and why the Boulevards are so wide. From the top of the Arc, there is a bird's-eye view across the rooftops but that is not all. Because the Arc was built at the centre of 12 mostly straight roads all radiating out, comme une etoile, your eyes are drawn to look beyond, or transcend across, all vistas of the city. C'est magnifique!

The monster of worry

Without wishing to denigrate the Arc in any way, which I still view as one of the seven wonders of the modern world, the Arc illustrates and enables me to reflect on worry. The Arc is huge if viewed from the outside, just as worry can be huge.

The Arc seems indestructible just as worry looks indestructible. The often said "Don't worry" might at times be like telling someone to tear down the Arc de Triomphe with bare hands! The 158 battles etched into the stonework seem to represent the many battles fought against worry. The tomb of the Unknown Soldier seems to represent the loneliness of worry. Yet the Arc represents something even more tragic.

It was never to be the triumphant arch as intended. This caused me to consider just how much time is spent devoted to building huge "worried monuments" in the mind that serve no purpose. All moments spent worrying are wasted moments. All the anguish and hand wringing gets nowhere! Worry is never triumphant. It is tragic.

There is yet another comparison that can be made with worry experienced by those who want to make their way to the top. This is the struggle with the seemingly everlasting 280 winding steps. They are dark, claustrophobic, crowded, exhausting and obstructive. A perfect description of worry. Yet it is the way to the top and many seem to want and compete to get to the top. It seems to reflect life.

For many years, I worked as a member of a professional body in the City of London. In my latter years leading up to retirement, I used to train graduate trainees to sit a test of competence. They needed to pass this before they could apply for membership of the professional body. I have always enjoyed working with young people so it will be of no surprise to say that I found the experience to be both rewarding and uplifting. It did have one drawback however and that was their fear of failure. I have no criticism of the competence test as an examination system any more than I wish to denigrate the Arc de Triomphe. It represents a challenge in life and the test is a big hurdle for the graduates to jump. It comprises a ten-minute presentation followed by a 50-minute oral examination. Worry grew in the weeks leading up to the event. Sometimes worry became monumental. Occasionally there were tears. My job was to get the graduates to face the challenge and overcome it. I reflected that for most it was like climbing those winding stairs in the Arc.

But what joy when they passed! They had made it. For a sporadic moment, they are content. They could now look out to new horizons in their professional life. For a brief moment, it was like being on top of the world and yet they knew, as we all know, that before long they would be at the bottom again, facing worry about another exhausting climb. For many, this is the cycle of life. Yet Paul writes to the church at Philippi, "Don't be anxious about anything".

Toward transcending

I confess that at first sight what Paul writes in Philippians 4:6, "don't be anxious about anything" is like aiming a popgun at the Arc de Triomphe! Over the past two years, I have challenged Christians in particular with, "Do not be anxious about anything" The response can vary from a shrug, a pleasant tolerant smile or a look of utter disbelief. I do not believe that Paul ever meant this statement to be read in isolation. It is part of a larger unit. We should look at it with what is around it. I do not wish to give offence to anyone but we might look at it in the same way as we might look at a hamburger. Imagery can sometimes be useful particularly when looking at something difficult. Perhaps it might help if I write Philippians 4:4–7 out this way:

(Top bun) *Rejoice in the Lord always.*
I will say it again, Rejoice
Let your gentleness be evident to all.

(Meat and relish)*The Lord is near*
<u>*Do not be anxious about anything.*</u>

(bottom bun) *but in everything by prayer and petition*
with thanksgiving
present your requests to God.

(guarantee of satisfaction) *And the peace of God*
which transcends all understanding
will guard your hearts
and your minds in Christ Jesus.

Top Bun. We are to start with a positive state of mind and indeed we have something to be positive about. We have begun a journey to transcend or look beyond worry. So rejoice. Do not start out defeated. Have a gentle disposition toward ourselves and a kindly disposition to others.

Meat and relish. "Don't be anxious about anything," is the meat at the centre of the dish. This is the nourishment. It is the sustenance that gives us strength and support as we go about our daily lives. However, just the meat in the bun is not enough. It needs what many would consider the best bit of the burger – the relish. "The Lord is near" – that is the relish. This is the taste that we never forget. We experience times when the Lord is near and never forget the taste even when he seems far, far away. David, the King of Israel, understood this when he wrote his remarkable Psalm 23, "Even though I walk through the Valley of the Shadow of Death, you are with me." (v4)

Bottom bun. The bottom layer is prayer. "But in everything by prayer and petition with thanksgiving present your requests to God." We come to God in humility, knowing our dependence on him for our very salvation and transcending worry is part of that salvation. In humility, we discern that God created us not to worry but to pray. When we pray we are never isolated. Worry is a lonely place but we are never alone in prayer. Our prayer time may or may not be with other people, but God is always present.

Guarantee of satisfaction. This is a promise. "And the peace of God which transcends all understanding will guard your hearts and your minds in Christ Jesus." These words are often used in the blessing at the end of a church service. They send us out into the world in a positive frame of mind. This "burger" is the best. "Taste and see that the Lord is good. Blessed is the man who takes refuge in him," Psalm 34:8. Armed with this knowledge and understanding, we can begin our journey toward transcending worry not in our own feeble strength but in the strength of the One who guards our hearts and minds.

Transcending worry

Looking back I can recall an early event in my Christian life when all this seemed to come together. When I was in my early 30s, I was asked to produce an Easter play for the church that I was attending at the time. The play chosen was *Christ in the Concrete City* by Phillip Turner. Now this was not a church, you might say, that was steeped in a prayer tradition. We would take Holy Communion faithfully each week but meeting together to pray was quite unheard of. I had not been attending this church for long so the people there did not know me well. In spite of this, I was at a meeting where there was an intention that I produce the play. I protested vigorously. "I have never produced a play before," I remonstrated, "Actually I have never acted in one either". My faith was being tested but they insisted. I continued to protest, "You won't even like the way that I will produce this play," I pleaded.

"Why won't we?" they questioned.

"Because I will insist that we pray before each rehearsal and performance." They did not hesitate. I was voted in!

The production had its challenges. The cast of four men and two women were sometimes disciples, sometimes part of a crowd or sometimes part of a chorus – that is the six actors talking as one. At times one became Mary Magdalen or another Simon Peter. The problem was how could I, as producer who never had produced a play before, choreograph this play so that the audience would know who the actors were playing or what they were doing at any one time. The author's written score was only the words that the actors spoke and there were few directions. This caused great head scratching. I wrestled with it day and night and at times it would keep me awake as I figured out each and every move and action that I wanted the actors to make.

I do not think I dwelt on a moment of worry while I produced that project. No hand wringing. No wondering whether we would get the production off the ground on time. No wishing I had never taken it on. On the contrary, this would rank as one of my most creative achievements. Yes, I had wrestled and lost sleep and worried thoughts came into my mind but we were intent on displaying a work about Christ crucified. The Lord was near during the whole project and we never failed to pray before each rehearsal and performance. It was "wrapped" in faith and prayer. We transcended worry even when an elderly member of the cast lost the sight in one eye during one of the rehearsals and carried on without telling anyone! We looked beyond the problems to the finished production. We did it once and the following year, we did it twice more – even better.

Of course, this was a big step right out of our comfort zones but most of the steps to transcend worry are small. We have faith in God who is near even when everything is falling apart. Much has to be learned and much has to be endured. The end result is a goal worth achieving as we look beyond to the one who guards our hearts and minds. It like reaching the roof of the Arc, gasping for breath and looking out over the city.

Worry is under our feet and we look at life – this life and eternal life stretching out before us.

In the meantime, the church at Philippi was ordered to stand firm in the Lord. Stand firm against what? Against worry of course.

CHAPTER TWO
STANDING FIRM

The Lord is near.
Philippians 4:5

As our Bible passage from Philippians 4:1–13 comes toward the end of the letter that Paul sent to the Macedonian church, I need to give it some context as to what has gone before. My purpose is not to look at the whole letter, so setting the passage into context will be necessarily brief. Yet I think that this is possible because, to me, the first three chapters (indeed the whole letter) hinge on a most beautiful creed in Philippians 2. I remember most distinctly first reading this creed at a house party when I was a very young Christian in my early 20s, so I make no apologies for setting it out in full. Paul exhorts the Philippians:

Your attitude should be the same as that of Jesus Christ.
Who, being in the very nature God
did not consider equality with God
something to be grasped
but made himself nothing
taking the very nature of a servant
being made in human likeness
and being found in appearance as a man.
He humbled himself
and became obedient to death – even death on a cross.
Therefore God exalted him to the highest place

and gave him the name that is above every name.
That at the name of Jesus every knee should bow
in heaven and on earth and under the earth
and every tongue confess that Jesus Christ is Lord
to the glory of God the Father. (Philippians 2:5–11)

Take a moment to look at this creed. I love it for its simplicity. Being a creed, it is a statement of faith and can be divided into two parts. The last part of the creed is devoted to the majesty of Jesus whereby our faith is in an Almighty God who is bigger than our worry. The first part is devoted to our faith in following the qualities of Jesus in the world that might be summed up as follows:

Our faith is in Jesus
who made himself nothing taking
the very nature of a servant.
Faith, humility and service.

Now if we look at Paul's letter to the Philippian church, we can see that it follows this summary:

- In Philippians 1, Paul expresses his **faith** in Jesus – "to live is Christ, to die is gain" (Philippians 1:21).
- In Philippians 2, Paul expresses his **humility** in Jesus– "Do everything without complaining or arguing" (Philippians 2:14).
- In Philippians 3 Paul is at God's **service** in Jesus. Paul presents his CV to the Philippians. As for format, it is the same as any of the hundreds of CVs that I have seen in my working years. He says what he is, followed by what he wants to achieve. The difference here is that Paul's CV is for one person only – Jesus Christ. "I want to know Christ and the power of his resurrection" (Philippians 3:10). That is it and no other. When he met Jesus on the Damascus Road, everything that went before changed. Now he is

wholly in the service of Jesus. Nothing was more important to Paul than this. "I press on towards the goal to win the prize to which God has called me heavenward in Christ Jesus" (Philippians 3:14).

Paul exhorts the young church (see Philippians 4:9) to put into practice what they have learned, received or heard from him or seen in him. Faith, humility and service in Jesus. These are the keystones for someone who in Jesus is transcending worry and who now, in Jesus, is progressing toward finding the secret of being "content in any and every situation" (Philippians 4:12). With this, I can present the structure of this book, for having examined the means Paul gives us to transcend worry (Chapters 4–10), we will finish (chapters 11–14) by finding "the secret" through faith, humility and service in Jesus.

Having read the first three chapters of Philippians, we reach our passage in Philippians 4 and we come down to earth with a bump. There is a monumental bust-up! Paul got to hear about it 615 miles away in prison in Rome. Euodia and Syntyche are the names of two ladies in the church of Philippi who quarrelled. We do not know what the row was about nor do we know whether it was a blazing set-to or a simmering feud. Paul implored the church to "help these women who have contended at my side." (v1) Considering this, these two ladies were probably pillars of the church and possibly of the community, yet we know nothing of the good things that they may have done. We only know that they quarrelled. What a shame! Is this not a lesson to all who might get involved in church quarrels? Would we only want to be remembered for our part in a brouhaha? Just something to think about.

We meet some other members of the church. There's "loyal yokefellow", somebody with no title but who worked both anonymously and loyally, recognised by those who read the letter at Philippi. We meet "Clement and the rest of my co-workers" (v3) Was Clement a leader in the church? I think this might be likely as his name is singled-out. Clement means merciful which seems just right for the moment. These, along with the women, were the people whom Paul loved and longed for.

So the scene is set for the morning when the letter arrives. Let us, just for a moment, consider what the church at Philippi might have thought as Clement excitedly opened this letter from their founder and mentor, while the co-workers gathered around. They read about his faith in what we now call chapter one. Perhaps they marvelled at the beauty of the creed in chapter two. In chapter three, Paul presents his CV hardly worthy of any prize, yet through his faith in Jesus, he presses on heavenward to win the prize. If he can do it, they can do it and, in the same way, we can do it. Then they get to the quarrel between the women in chapter 4 and their hearts might have plummeted.

Stand firm in the Lord, dear friends. – Well... er... OK we will give it a go. And then...

Rejoice in the Lord – What have we got to rejoice about? We are stuck in a feud.

... and again I say rejoice! – (Paul seemed to know exactly how they would react)

Let your gentleness be evident to all. – But... but... Paul no amount of gentleness is going to sort out THIS altercation.

The Lord is near – Yes but where?

Do not be anxious about anything – Are you serious?

So I think that it is quite possible that this letter might have initially received a similar response to the one that we might have when we try to give serious attention to "Do not be anxious about anything". However, this is a letter of love. Paul is not writing to them with a curt "Stop worrying!" He is writing with loving tears in his eyes telling them to stand firm in the Lord and help these ladies. Perhaps not what they wanted to hear. There are times when God calls us to stand firm. I recall a time when I had to face that challenge – a challenge I did not want to receive.

Standing wobbly in the Lord

"Hiya John," said the voice at the end of the telephone, "how about meeting me at the Bosun and Call tonight at 7.30. I'll buy you a beer". Nothing unusual about that but it came from my then vicar (not Saju but many vicar's before him) All unsuspecting, I arrived at the pub at the allotted time only to be told, once the pint was in my hand, that he was moving on to another job and... would I take over as churchwarden!

"The problem is", he cheerily announced, "there is a faction within the church that might rear its head before you get a new vicar".

This was not what I wanted to hear. Oh well, perhaps the interregnum will be short. Perhaps "the faction" will stay quiet. The interregnum was not short and "the faction" did not stay quiet. In that moment at the Bosun and Call, clutching my pint of beer and looking at my then vicar happily grinning at me as we contemplated our new challenges... I was being asked to stand firm in the Lord.

The problems arising from "the faction" could have come in several different ways. It manifested itself eventually in the youth club. My fellow churchwarden and I were becoming increasingly uneasy about what was being taught there so, with heart in mouth, we decided to close it down to be reviewed by the new vicar when he arrived. I told the youth club leaders of our decision and in church next Sunday morning, it was clear that World War III had broken out!

"The faction" was on the rampage and people were listening to them. That night I went to bed and woke up feeling like I was sleeping in a bed of ice. I suddenly remembered that we were approaching the AGM. I, and my fellow warden, were going to be hung out to dry!

Then a week before the AGM, I received a telephone call from the Archdeacon. "John I'm coming to your AGM," he said.

"Why are you doing that?" I asked.

"To chair it of course," he replied as if I should have known.

I was overwhelmed with relief. The evening of the AGM arrived. The presence of the Archdeacon clearly upended "the faction". The Archdeacon, fully aware of everything, led the meeting with an utter lack of concern. Then came a moment when "the faction" tried to disturb the otherwise calmness of the proceedings but the Archdeacon dealt with it with great gentleness. A stranger coming into the meeting would not have known that any sort of problem existed.

And all I had to do was stand! I did not have to say a word except to stand and thank the Archdeacon for coming. I stood and I made myself vulnerable and it was scary. Then everything else fell into place. "The faction" made peace with me. One by one, they came to me days and weeks after the AGM, asking my advice or just for a chat. We handed the church over to a new vicar (with great relief) and the youth club was eventually re-opened.

I have reflected back on this event many times since it happened because something didn't completely stack up with standing firm in the Lord. I stood up that night and I had stood up in the Lord but, to be utterly honest... I wasn't really standing firm. Yes, I was amazed as I saw the opposition drop away but truthfully, I cannot claim to be anything other than feeling very wobbly. Standing wobbly in the Lord did not seem quite right! The problem was that I was anxious...I was worried.

Jesus deals with wobbliness

So I turned to Jesus with a question. Did Jesus have wobbly moments? I don't think I could ever imagine that he did. Yet, as the creed in Philippians 2 makes clear, he was created all-human as well as all-god. If he was all-human then he must have had wobbly moments because, I think I am safe to say, even the most grounded humans will experience wobbly moments sometime in their lives. Looking at the gospels, I have found two occasions when Jesus seemed to have had a wobble.

The first is a very John-sort-of-everyday-wobble. What is for supper? There are times when Sally can get quite exasperated with this wobble. However although I might not know what is for supper, I can be relatively confident that there will be supper. Not so for Jesus. He was in the desert. He was hungry and there was no sign of any food or the means of obtaining food. With prolonged hunger and heat his mind might have started doing funny tricks. The very stones that he was walking on, worn rounded by centuries of desert wind, began to take on the appearance of bread. The temptation to contemplate this illusion would have been great but Jesus batted it off. Referring to his humanity, he said, "Man does not live on bread alone but on every word that comes from the mouth of God" (Matt 4:4).

The second occasion was a wobbliness that was devastating. Jesus was facing his death. It was not to be an ordinary death but it would be hideously painful, prolonged and humiliating. Worse still, no one around him remotely understood. He was in the Garden of Gethsemane the night before his crucifixion when he became overwhelmed with sorrow. He fell flat on his face and prayed, "My Father, if it is possible, may this cup be taken from me" (Matt 26:39). That has to be a wobbly moment, doesn't it? But, immediately Jesus adds with great humility "yet not as I will but as you will".

To me, these stories say two things. Firstly, Jesus had wobbly moments. To deny this would be to deny his all-human nature. Secondly, and more importantly, it is what he did with these wobbly moments. In both cases, he immediately turned away from his feelings and concentrated on God who he knew was near. He was standing firm. He suffered the wobbly moment but he did not carry it. Instead, God was near and he stood firmly against it. This is what Paul was saying to Clement and Co. Face the problem, stand firm in the Lord. But how? At times, that seems far from being straightforward.

Standing firm in the Lord

Like everybody else, Saju has wobbly moments. He told me of one big wobbly moment which he faced with the help of his loving wife. This is what he told me:

> "At the end of my curacy I had to look for a job as a vicar or priest-in-charge of a church. I made application to a church that I knew in the north of England not far from where Katy and I were living with our four children. It was a large church and they were looking for an associate vicar with the expectation that I would take over the role of vicar. It did not work out and I was left like many flung onto the jobs market looking for a Living, always in competition with others. The problem is that I am no good at writing. I can talk, I can exhort – but writing is not my forte. Application after application met a dead end. All very depressing and all very understandable to many. I began to sense that the Church of England did

not want me and I began to look at other denominations. It was in this worried confusion that Katy arranged for me to spend some time in Israel. I walked the streets of Jerusalem, visited Bethlehem and toured Galilee – all the time reading the Gospels affirming the place with the written word. It was a starting point. I began to stand firm in the realisation that I was loved by Jesus and that my value did not come with affirmation from other people, rather, it came from knowing that Jesus was standing firm with me. I learned that lesson where Jesus walked and it has stayed with me ever since."

Saju saw the desert where Jesus walked weak and hungry. He saw the Garden where Jesus prayed flat on his face. He saw the way through to standing firm as Jesus did. He found his answer by turning the issue completely around. Instead of trying to stand firm against a sea of interviews or a nagging doubt that the Church of England did not want him, he chose to look beyond those things and see Jesus, far bigger than worry, standing firm with him. Jesus the name above all names. This realisation bought him to the south of the country to be my vicar for a time and from there to become a Bishop!

What Saju did was to transcend worry. I think that is admirable and, knowing Saju, I know his faith and contemplative mind would have bought him through this difficult time. We are all different and I am not sure that it would work for me. Actually, I did not think anything would enable me to combat worry. Oblivious of what was to come, I sat one Sunday morning in church not knowing that God was going to challenge me with this familiar passage from Philippians 4. A passage, which I admired for its beauty, but which I had discarded in my heart.

CHAPTER THREE
REPLACE

The peace of God which transcends
all understanding Philippians 4:7

It was the word "replace" that bought me out of my spiritual slumber that morning not long before the first covid lockdown. Matt, our lay leader, was preaching on our passage from Philippians 4. I was sitting in the congregation at the time supposedly listening to Matt, but if truth be known, my attention was more self-indulgent. I had heard it all before.

"Rejoice in the Lord always and again I say rejoice! Let your gentleness be evident to all. The Lord is near"(v4–5). I smiled within my self-detachment but it was not a smile of joy but it was more one of resignation.

"Such a beautiful passage," I mused, "How many times have I heard it read?"

"Do not be anxious about anything" (v6). I looked at the large cross at the front of the hall where we were worshipping. Ah yes, I thought – that bit of scripture but I have been a worrier all my life. My friends and family all know that I am a worrier. I regularly get teased about it. I am always half glass empty but it is all good humoured.

"... but in everything by prayer and petition with thanksgiving, present your requests to God"(v6). I continued in my self-indulgence. When did I, or anyone else, pray for my crippling sense of worry? I could not remember. This was no one's fault. No amount of prayer could shift my worry. Worry was so deep-seated within me. I could never see beyond it. I stifled a yawn.

"And the peace of God which transcends all understanding, will guard your hearts and your minds in Jesus Christ" (v7). I reflected sadly that my worried life had not always been a peaceful life. In spite of this, I had been a Christian for many years, and had held a licence from the bishop as a lay-reader. Later in life, God chose me through Saju to lay-lead our church in order to raise a new younger leadership. Now that task was completed and Matt had taken the helm with another team of leaders. Well God, why did you choose me? I continued to ponder not understanding just how near he was, there was much I didn't understand.

I felt that this passage from Philippians was like going into the Jewel House in the Tower of London to see the Crown Jewels. So beautiful – so unattainable. So close – within arm's reach – yet they are beyond reach. There is a thick transparent barrier that divides observers from the jewels preventing anybody physically holding their beauty. We can look, wonder, and think about what they are, who has worn them, where they have been worn but we can only observe and never hold.

"Whatever is true, whatever is noble, whatever is just, whatever is pure, whatever is lovely, whatever is commendable – if anything is excellent or praiseworthy, think about these things" (v8). My self-indulgence drew to a familiar conclusion. This list Paul wrote was a barrier to my comprehension. For me to try and think about this list puts this beautiful passage well beyond my reach. I mean (I'm talking to you God) do you really think that when I'm worried I can think about whatever is noble or whatever is pure etc. The list seemed beyond all understanding. I felt some sort of self-justification stirring within me. "Whatever you have learned or received or heard from me, or seen in me – put it into practice. And the God of Peace be with you all" (v9). Having calmed myself, I mentally turned away from this scripture as Matt continued to speak. It was then something happened. Matt said a word, "replace!"

It seemed that the Lord had drawn near, sitting right next to me nudging me with a holy elbow. Replace! Matt was not saying "Go from here and worry no more". He was not giving us the third degree by telling us all that worry is a sin because it shows that we do not trust God. No, thank God, he was using the word "Replace!" Worry was to be replaced with something else – replace it by thinking about whatever is true, noble, just, pure, lovely, commendable, excellent and praiseworthy. It was on the word "commendable" that I had a sudden "lightbulb moment". I re-collected two small books that I had in my possession that I had won at my school's prize-giving many years ago. This was something commendable. For a moment, I was doing what Paul urged the Philippians and all of us to do. Replace! Replace! It was all over in a flash leaving me with only the tiniest glimpse of a way forward in my understanding of this beautiful passage. I was still very uncertain how Paul's list might be used to overcome worry.

Matt's talk came to an end. I cannot remember anything else he said. All I could think about was that word "replace". The service finished and after a time of social interaction with new faces and with those that I love, I went home. I knew I had to look at these oh-so-familiar verses further, particularly the ones that gave me most trouble. "Finally whatever is true, whatever is noble (honourable), whatever is right (just), whatever is pure, whatever is lovely, whatever is admirable (commendable) – if anything is excellent or praiseworthy – think about such things" (v8).

The dawning of understanding

Once home, I settled down with my daybook (where most of my scribblings begin) and drew two columns. On the left column, I listed the seven virtues in Philippians 4:8. On the right, I listed my immediate thoughts on each. This is what emerged:

- TRUTH — But the truth worries me.
- NOBLE (HONOURABLE) — Being noble is not my forte.
- RIGHT (JUST) — There is no justice – that's the point.
- PURE — You've got to be joking!
- LOVELY — My wife and waterfalls.
- ADMIRABLE (COMMENDABLE) — I did think of something in church.
- EXCELLENT AND PRAISEWORTHY — If only...

It was an inauspicious yet unsurprising start. For a while, I wondered whether Paul had got the list right. Surely there must be other things to think about to replace worry. So I added some other "virtues" to the list:

- HOLIDAYS (FREEDOM) — Probably cause more worry than anything else.
- HUMOUR — Love humour but relief from worry is only fleeting.
- STRONG — Thinking myself as strong is a delusion.
- HAPPY — Too slippery.

"Rejoice. Let your gentleness be evident to all" (v5). It would have been very easy at that point to give up. However, I continued the process with a big dollop of gentleness particularly as things were not self-evident. Even so, it took a little while for the penny to drop but when it did, I realised that I was looking at the list in completely the wrong way. I was looking at the list with myself at the centre. Paul's list made no sense while I centred it on "me". Yet I have lived in a culture of "me" all of my life – what I want, what I need, what I deserve. I was looking at this passage like having a stick with a camera attached and spending time taking "selfies" of myself. "Me" in the picture; "me" at the centre.

I began to realise why I struggled with Philippians 4:1–13. "Me" had to come out. But if "me" isn't at the centre of the list, who is? I had to think some more. "Where did his journey to overcome worry begin?" An answer rolled into my mind. "It began in church two weeks before lock down when the Lord drew near".

Say that again!

It began when the Lord drew near.

Of course!

The list fits when applied to the Lord.

Look! The Lord is true, the Lord is noble, the Lord is just, the Lord is pure, the Lord is lovely, the Lord is commendable, the Lord is excellent and praiseworthy. "God" or "Jesus" or "the Lord" are connotations equally acceptable but the list does not work with "me". It would have been a perfect discussion point with Saju over a glass of burgundy, sitting by the River Seine. The only problem was that right then, we were on opposite sides of the world! This did not put me off. Through exchanges of emails, he told me that this list of God characteristics can be manifested through people. God's excellence shines in people. God's nobility shines through people. God's commendability works through people. What I was doing in my thinking was limiting my thoughts on this list to my own human smallness. My thinking had to be revised. At last, I had begun to wake up to the reality of this passage. "Think on these things" wrote Paul. Yes, I had to think.

Rejoice! Here is a way to transcend worry. Paul writes, "Do not be anxious about anything," and I baulk at that. He tells me to, "Stand firm in the Lord" and I baulk even more! Anxiety/worry brings me down. Standing firm makes me wobbly. But the Lord is near and the Lord has given not just to me but to everyone, a list of God-characteristics to think about in order to replace and thereby transcend worry. Where to start? I thought back to the church where I had had a "lightbulb moment" about two little books. Ah yes, I remember. Actually, that was about some very smelly cheese!

Smelly cheese

The opportunities at school to be awarded a prize were few-and-far between. Peter was very bright and won most of them. Nobody could compete with Peter. So how did I manage to win the prize for geography? Like everything else, it seemed, I was not particularly good at geography. It was all because of my dad. My dad was determined that I was going to win a commendation. He chose geography because he enjoyed geography. All I had to do was to go along with Dad. Dad did it all. He told me what we were going to do, he then researched what we did and then organised the presentation. All I had to do was say "yes Dad", and then write what he told me to write. I did have to exercise one thing, however. I had to have faith that what my dad was telling me was right and humbly be willing to go along with how he led me. I had that faith and humility. I just had to produce the service.

Dad decided that I was to present a project on English cheeses (my dad dearly loved cheese!). A presentation box with a lid was prepared, in which was placed a sample of every English cheese that we could get. There were only around 14 English cheeses back then. The project, along with the sample box of cheeses, sat at the back of the Geography Room at school with all the other projects presented. Time passed and the cheese began to stink. This presented a godsend for teenage boys who delighted in removing the lid from the box before lessons began, thus filling the room with the acrid smell of rotting cheese! Nevertheless, I won the prize. I walked out in front of the whole school along with parents, received the prize and the accolades. I treasure these two books – prizes that I won. When I thought of what is admirable or commendable, I thought of those books.

But – it should have been my dad who walked out before the school and received the prize, shouldn't it? He was the one that should be commended, the one to be admired – not me! With that admission, we have an illustration of how we might think about whatever is admirable, in fact how we might think about all these God-characteristics. My dad represented the Lord. My dad wanted to enable me to do something for which I would get a prize and be admired. It was OK for me to receive the prize because it was what my dad wanted. This is an illustration of the Lord. He wants his followers to serve him sometimes to complete tasks seemingly beyond reach and he wants to applaud us so that we might worship him. He wants to give us something to think about, contemplate and weigh up, replacing worry so that thoughts can transcend toward our admirable Lord and God.

Thinking and replacing

I was off the mark! I still had my daybook open in front of me so I listed the God characteristics on one side, as before but now on the other side, I considered what category of God-characteristic would fit my thoughts on smelly cheese.

TRUTH	My story is true enough but smelly cheese does not tell me much about the concept of truth.
NOBLE	My story could fit here. I think my dad showed great nobility
JUST	No, not much justice in this story. Dad did not get the prize. I did.
PURE	I have not worked this one out yet.
LOVELY	It is a lovely story but can I put smelly cheese into the category of 'lovely'?
ADMIRABLE	The story definitely fits here. Dad was admirable and I got the commendation.
EXCELLENT AND PRAISEWORTHY	God is excellent! God is praiseworthy!

I decided to put the story into the God-characteristic of ADMIRABLE but I realised that it could fit into other God-characteristics as well. Actually, it didn't matter where I put it. The important thing is that I was thinking about it and by thinking about it, I was replacing worry. I began to think of other stories and where I would place them.

It was then that I realised that there was a book aching to be born. Looking back, I can see how God drew me toward the book's conception some three years before in Paris when I was with Saju. Now was the time to write with the purpose of presenting an exercise which Paul encouraged the Philippians and all other worriers to do in order to replace worry. I could do that exercise with Saju's help. As can be seen from my composed list above, there were aspects about the passage that I still did not understand.

Therefore, it needs to be said, reading these thoughts in the following chapters will not magically enable others to transcend worry. These are my thoughts and they are written to encourage others to think for themselves and hopefully enable them to transcend worry. My thoughts have been arranged carefully in the chapters that follow. In actuality, my thoughts were scattered. They were like scraps of paper littering my apartment. They had to be gathered together and made into a cohesive pattern of both Bible stories and my own experiences along with the experiences of others.

I needed to do the exercise with someone else. Others may need to do the same. Saju, so different from me in age and culture, would both clarify and inspire my thoughts. We hit it off between us! Saju has moved on to others things but he left our church with the idea of "trios". This comprises groups of three men or three women who zoom periodically to discuss the Bible, pray and to share their own experiences. It is so important to know that we are not alone in our worried struggles.

My fragmented thoughts began to be pieced together making up a huge jigsaw puzzle and the picture that emerged was something much bigger than worry. It was a picture of the Lord. Jesus – the name above all names, to whom every knee shall bow, as the old creed observes. Even when problems hit me and health issues threatened to bring me down, I realised that Jesus was bigger. By replacing worry and thoughts of these great God-characteristics, I could look beyond worry to Jesus. I have my wobbly moments but I can "press on" as Paul wrote in Philippians 3:14, "towards the goal to win the prize which God has called me heavenwards in Christ Jesus".

Is this all true? I was about to consider this with Saju, thinking about whatever is true.

CHAPTER FOUR

THINKING ABOUT
WHATEVER IS TRUE

I am the way, the truth and the life. John 14:6

The Oxford Dictionary chose "Post-Truth" as their 2016 word of the year, which poses the question, how do we talk about truth in a Post-Truth world? Andrew Keen, the founder of the world's largest privately-owned public relations company, observed, "In this era of exploding media technologies there is no truth except the truth you create for yourself." The Silicon Valley entrepreneur calls it the "great seduction": The Web 2.0 revolution has peddled the promise of bringing more truth to more people – more depth of information, perspective that is more global, more unbiased opinion from dispassionate observers. But this is all a smokescreen... [the] chilling reality in this brave new digital epoch is the blurring, obfuscation, and even disappearance of truth. Quentin Schultze, Professor of Communication at Calvin College, agrees that the torrent of information now at our disposal is often little more than "endless volleys of nonsense, folly, and rumour masquerading as knowledge, wisdom, and even truth." Masking the truth will have an inevitable consequence. People will worry.

Ryhard Bonnke, the German-American evangelist, in his book *Evangelism By Fire* writes, "The modern media pours moral pollution into the atmosphere like chimneys belting smoke.

We need a gas mask not to breathe in the soul diseases of a materialistic age, with its accompanying unbelief". The media had a field day through covid lockdown. Every morning the news greeted us with statistics and speculation. At times, it seemed to the eyes and ears of this viewer, that those invited to be interviewed were in some form of competition as to who could be the gloomiest. We seemed always to get the worst scenario. People I talked to often told me that they had stopped watching the news as it fuelled their worries.

I asked Sally who is a therapeutic counsellor about truth. The vast majority of her clients recognise that worry and anxiety are major problems in their lives. However, the majority of these worries are based on perceptions in clients' minds that might be untrue. Yet these possible untruths have been accepted and believed, and have thus become a source of irrational worry. A hypothetical example representing this type of difficulty might be a person concerned about their managerial role in the workplace. Whilst managing their work to the satisfaction of their line managers, worries emerge on how their colleagues perceive them. Without any clear evidence, a conclusion might be reached, that colleagues hold negative perceptions that in turn adds to the worries already in their lives. Such a thought pattern may have built up over many years, and they believe that others see them in this negative light. This colours their whole life and personal relationships and undermines their self-esteem. Don't we just want something or somebody dependable to hold on to?

The Truth is a man

"We (Christians) believe that the Truth is a man". Saju was in full spate as the two of us started thinking about the truth but I had stopped listening to him any further. Instead, I was thinking about what he had just said. It kept ringing in my ears. "We believe The Truth is a man". How can that be? Surely not? However before I asked Saju these questions, a thought flashed through my mind. Actually, there is a verse in the Bible that was so familiar and was ingrained in my memory. It was one of Jesus' great I AMs "I am the Way, the Truth and the Life" (John 14:6).

How many times had I heard that preached and yet not internalised it? How could I be taken aback when someone presents Jesus' teaching so simply? So I decided, mischievously perhaps, to try it out on some Christian friends of long standing. When the moment was right, I would lob into a discussion, "The Truth is a man". Then I noted, with some satisfaction, how they also hesitated as I had done, their minds going into a contemplative spiral.

"I am the Truth." This was no tub-thumping exercise from Jesus saying "Look at me. This is who I am". Rather this is Jesus comforting his disciples. He had just told them that he was going away and they were upset. So he gives them a "rock" on which they could depend – "I am The Way, the Truth and the Life," he said. God knows all things. He is the Alpha and the Omega – the beginning and the end. He knows when we are born and when we die. "Indeed, the very hairs on your head are numbered" (Luke 12:7). – I'm always amused by that verse because the implication is that it does not take much to know me!! Jesus is God come into the world. All Truth is vested in him. The Truth is that God's chosen way is through Jesus who can lead us to God and to eternal life. Oh, what did we do with the Truth while he was with us, living among us? What did we do?

What is Truth?

"What is truth?" Pontius Pilate asked Jesus famously at a time when he was very worried. Jerusalem was in chaos and chaos

53

would not impress the Emperor Tiberius. Pilate's job was to subdue the troublesome province – not incite it to riot. Yet incitement to riot was what might result unless he carried out the wishes of the Jewish leaders and authorise a crucifixion. He decided to examine the prisoner.

Jesus, standing before him, said to Pilate, "I came into the world to testify to the truth. Everyone on the side of truth listens to me" (John 18:37). This prompted Pilate to ask his famous question "What is truth?" which might be considered one of the sharpest questions we have in the Gospels. However, having asked the great question, Pilate did not stop to listen to Jesus' response. He walked out. As one commentator says, Pilate squandered the opportunity of a lifetime for a rhetorical punch line. It made for a dramatic exit, but a pitiful display. John's gospel has already told us what Jesus' reply would have been had he stopped to listen.

However, Pontius Pilate walked out on The Truth, he then decided to flog The Truth before presenting the bloodied Truth to the mob. "Ecce homo!" he said, "Behold the man!" (John 19:5 KJV). It is a scene that has imprinted itself on many great artists, including Rembrandt and Caravaggio. The sight of a bloodied and wounded Jesus was like holding a mirror up to the crowd. The man standing before them was Jesus, The Truth, and they recoiled. They were looking at their own brokenness. At that fateful moment, Pilate might, had he listened, equally have shouted, "Behold the Truth!" but they screamed "Crucify him!" (John 19 :6). That day they crucified Jesus and humankind has been crucifying The Truth before and ever since. Deitrich Bonhoeffer, pastor, theologian and anti-nazi dissident, was absolutely right when he wrote "The cross is God's truth about us, and therefore it is the only power which can make us truthful."

What crowd?

It was early evening one Monday and I was consumed in thought about this chapter. Sally broke into my deep contemplation telling me what they were planning the following morning in their "trio" meeting (for "trio" meetings see chapter three). I have to confess that I had to suppress feelings of irritation that she had interrupted my wrestling. However when I turned my attention to what she was saying, I realised that she was referring to Acts, chapter two and the story of what happened at Pentecost several weeks after the crucifixion. Situation – same city/different crowd. Peter, who was filled with the Holy Spirit of God along with the eleven disciples stood and raised his voice addressing the crowd – and he didn't pull his punches. We are told in Acts 2:37 that the people were, "cut to the heart and cried out to Peter and the other apostles 'What shall we do?'"

So we have within a few weeks of each other, two crowds gathered together in the same city whilst celebrating a great

Jewish feast, yet we see two quite different reactions. One crowd screamed, "Crucify him" whilst the other crowd was repentant. I am just going to pose a very simple question. Which crowd are we in? Some may say that they want nothing to do with Jesus, that his very name is offensive or that they remain quite indifferent as they have not really thought about it and really do not want to. They would all be in the "Crucify him" group. The other group would comprise those who have accepted Jesus as Lord. He is the Truth. This group would call themselves Christians. However, I think that there is a third group and this might be quite a large group. The third group is the "don't know" group. Those who think that they perhaps might belong to both groups. I confess that, facing up to the truth, I might be in the "don't know" group – even as a self-confessed Christian. Sometimes I am in one group and then there are times when I am in another. I reached this recognition about myself through a troubling passage in John's gospel chapter 8 vv31-42.

The truth shall set you free

Jesus was speaking to another crowd, or maybe more of a group, and these were, "Jews who had believed him" (8:31) and he gives them a fantastic promise, "If you hold to my teaching you are really my disciples. Then you will know the truth and the truth will set you free" (8:31–32). But – there was no applause. Instead, it gave great offence.

"Set us free. What does he mean 'set us free'?"

"We are already free."

"We descended from Abraham."

"We are Jews."

"How dare he imply we are not free!"

"Preposterous!" (Taken from John 8:33-41).

After their protestations, Jesus then said in 8:40, "As it is you are determined to kill me, a man who has told you the truth that I heard from God" – and these were people who believed in him. Now they want to kill him! Did Jesus mean kill him physically or kill what he had to say? I am not sure and I do not think it matters. They wanted to shut him up. "Crucify him!"

I have to confess that I tend to do the same. I am OK with Jesus if all is going well. I am OK while I think that he is blessing me in what I am doing. I am OK if I think I am walking in his Truth. But the moment that things go wrong, I'm screaming "Foul! – It's not fair! – crucify him!". And then later, when I have calmed down, I return to "the other crowd" and ask for his forgiveness. Let me finish this chapter with a story that illustrates this as we consider truthfully, what crowd we are in. It all happened while on my way to meet what looked like a giant food mixer!

The giant food mixer

On 4 July 2001, a urology consultant told me I had cancer. After some deliberation, it was felt that the best course of action was to have radiotherapy treatment at the Royal Marsden Hospital in Kensington. I made my way to South Kensington Tube Station and from there walked through the leafy suburbs of SW3 to my rendezvous with what I would describe as a giant food mixer. I would lay within its claws for about half an hour every week! On one particular week, I was feeling quite low. It so happened that I was in plenty of time and so, surprisingly, I popped into a church that was open. The church was full of activity thronged mainly with men who were getting a bowl of soup or a snack to eat or playing chess or draughts or just talking and reading.

I plucked up courage and went up to the doorman and asked whether there was anyone who could pray with me. This caused a bit of a kerfuffle that really centred on a lady who clearly was happy to pray with me but who needed a chaperone. Eventually one was found, who happened to be a young girl. Off the three of us went into a room where a chair was found for me and then the two women knelt one on my left and the other on my right. They asked me what I wanted prayer for and then they began to pray. Soon tears began to flow down my cheeks as I sobbed out my story. A city-based professional who daily dealt in millions of pounds, who rubbed shoulders with the movers and shakers – now humbled. All pride had gone as I sat sobbing in the presence of Jesus. Then the beautiful young girl said something that will never forget, "John, you are the apple of God's eye". I dried my eyes, got up, and thanked them both and then went off to my designated appointment with the giant food mixer.

I went off knowing two truths. The first truth was to accept that I had cancer. I had now got fed up with being disgruntled. I was now tired of yelling "crucify him" or joining the ranks of those who continually ask, "If God is a God of love then why suffering?" There were no answers there. So sitting between these two Christian souls, I humbly returned to repentance where I knew that God would forgive me and receive me back. The second truth was to know that God cared for me as his child that I was the "apple of his eye". To know that Jesus had drawn near and that his spirit would sustain me. The cancer stayed dormant within me for 21 years and those years would rank as some of the best years of my life.

Prayer: *Lord of all truth, help us to trust you when we struggle with the truth. Help us to put our faith in you when we are tempted to make up our versions of the truth, help us to be humble as you are when it comes to accepting the truth and, with accepting that you are the truth, bring us into your peace.*

Questions you might like to consider:

- What is the significance of truth in an anxious world?
- How do you see the truth as personified in Jesus?
- Is there a Bible verse that helps you think about the truth?
- Has learning or seeing truth given you peace?
- What thoughts would you include if you wrote this chapter on whatever is true?

CHAPTER FIVE

THINKING ABOUT WHAT IS NOBLE AND HONOURABLE

But noble people make noble plans and
by noble deeds they stand
Isaiah 32:8

Paul writes in our passage from Philippians, "Yes and I ask you loyal yokefellow, help these women" (4:3). Who is this loyal yokefellow? The answer is that we do not know but the church at Philippi would know who Paul is referring to. For my part, I tend to overlook "loyal yokefellow". In fact, to be absolutely truthful, I'm not sure that I have even noticed him before (or, maybe, it's a her). This speaks volumes about noble people. Paul is asking us to think of the unsung and noble. The ordinary and honourable. So "loyal yokefellows" whoever and wherever you are – this chapter honours you.

Excitement at the Great Sanhedrin

You could cut the atmosphere with a knife in the Great Sanhedrin chamber. Things were not looking too rosy for the two fishermen who had healed a crippled man, known to many, who regularly sat at the gate leading into the temple. Having done that, they then had the temerity to proclaim the cross and resurrection that had made the miracle possible. Ranged against them were the high priest with members of his family together with the rulers, elders and teachers of the law. The fishermen, who had been arrested and imprisoned overnight, now stood before the assembly of the great and good alongside the man who had been healed. It was true – this was going to be a one-sided affair – only not the way it seemed. For ranged against the Sanhedrin were Peter, John, the Holy Spirit, together with the evidence of the man who had been crippled. The popular acclamation that a miracle had occurred was a headache to them. One thing became clear very quickly. The Sanhedrin did not stand a chance!

They fell silent. The high priest solemnly asked the prisoners, "By what power or what name did you do this?" (Acts 4:7) What a gift question! Peter and John with the Holy Spirit did not waste a moment. It was a moment to honour God. "It is by the name of Jesus Christ of Nazareth whom you crucified but whom God raised from the dead, that this man stands before you healed" (Acts 4:10). What followed was pure farce! The assembly was stunned. These were just ordinary people. How could they possibly...? But the evidence was there. They all knew this crippled man because they, and many others, had passed by him at the gate many times going into the temple. There he was in front of them, grinning like a Cheshire cat, hopping from one previously crippled foot to the other and possibly throwing a few knowing winks at those who threw money into his pot. So what did they do? They did what meetings often do when stuck – they adjourned! But the ever-growing pressure from the populace meant that they couldn't shelve it for long and so, saving as much dignity as possible, they released the prisoners. (you can read the full text of the story in Acts 4:1–21)

These fishermen transcended from the truth of healing the beggar to giving honour to the nobility of God. They were just ordinary people and, in turn, God crowned them with honour. This represents the pattern of our church worship. Putting it simply, God wants us to honour him in our worship, so that he, in turn, can bring honour to each of us. If we depart church each week without feeling honoured by God, then something might have gone wrong with our worship. Take a moment to consider what a Danish philosopher has to say about this.

God is the audience

"God is the audience" – the words rang out. I was in the audience listening and observing Saju who was standing in front of the assembled church dressed in a flamboyant top, red trousers and Doc Martin boots. He was expounding on the teaching of the Danish philosopher Soren Kierkegaard who promoted the concept that western church worship was all wrong. Since medieval times, worshippers were only expected to observe. Kierkegaard produced a different model. Congregations are the actors: church leaders are the prompters; and God is the audience! Worship is to honour and pay homage to the nobility of God. "Yours Lord is the greatness and the power and the glory and the majesty and the splendour for everything in heaven and earth is yours" (1 Chronicles 29:11). While God is watching, appreciating... and applauding.

It follows that, if the congregation are the actors in worshipping the nobility of God, then whatever role each worshipper is destined to play is a high honour whatever that role may be. God is worthy of this honour and each worshipper undertaking a role in honouring God, will undertake a duty which will probably come at a sacrificial cost. Duty and sacrifice are the pillars of nobility. No one should go unnoticed in the congregation. The role-played to honour God with duty and sacrifice will, at times, transcend people beyond their self-believed limitations.

I recall a time when I was leading a confirmation class. Amongst those in the class were a lovely middle-aged couple, she was quite gregarious and outgoing whereas her husband was very shy. At some point I said something along the lines of, "None of us can be certain what God has in store. You never know – you might be asked one day to lead up at the front of church just as I do". Unknowingly I nearly lost two beloved members of the congregation! The couple revealed to me long afterwards that, when they got home, the husband was very upset at the mere suggestion that he would ever, ever, be standing at the front of the church before the congregation. "If that's the plan, I'm never going to go to church again let alone be confirmed," he complained to his wife. A few years later God honoured him when he became churchwarden!

Listening to Saju I realised that this pattern of discipleship is played out over and over again. A huge mistake is made by the church if it depends on the same people to do "God's work". God's honour is not just for the few. Church leaders are the prompters who, with God's direction, have the responsibility of raising up new people to find their roles in honouring God. God chooses ordinary people to honour him. The paradox is that these out-of-comfort moments are often exciting and memorable as people trust in the Holy Spirit, as the fishermen did, and find that they can achieve goals hitherto thought impossible.

"For when I am weak then I am strong" (Paul writing to the church in Corinth. 2 Corinthians 12:10),

Noble, ordinary people

Covid years have been difficult for many, but they produced many examples of nobility. Ordinary people going about their daily work in a sacrificial way and being honoured for their sacrifice. The doctors and nurses living sacrificial lives working long hours, putting their duty above all in order to help the sick. That is noble. Then there are others. Carers in residential homes, prison officers, police, postal workers, teachers – the list can go on.

One noble ambulance driver living a life of sacrifice and duty related how she had driven down streets where people were clapping outside their front doors or leaning out of their windows. She laughed as she recalled sounding their siren to entertain the children.

Another noble lady who works in a food store is a real character. Her mood is a lottery. Sometimes she is happy and chatty and at other times she is miserable, yet getting to know her is getting to respect, laugh and like her the way she is. Walking home one day some neighbours stopped and clapped her as she walked passed. She had had yet another hard day, running the risk of infection, particularly while shop managers were trying to get their heads around what had to be done to contain the virus in their stores. Her face, often so downcast, was wreathed in smiles as she saw and heard the appreciation of what she was doing.

None of these people would describe themselves as being influential or wise by human standards. These ordinary people were fully aware of the difficulties before them and the risks they were taking in doing their jobs. Probably they would have been worried in some way or other. So to encourage them during April and May in 2020 every Thursday at 8.00pm, communities came to their front doors to clap frontline workers, doing exactly what Paul is urging all to do. The effect of honouring these workers was to think about what is "noble". People were enacting what is written in Philippians 4 whether or not they knew the Bible passage. "Do not be anxious about anything... whatever is noble or honourable... think about such things".

"Are you OK, Tamsin?" asked Sally to a young mother after a church zoom service. Tamsin had sat quiet and had said nothing. The church knew that she worked in maternity. "How are things at the hospital, Tamsin?" asked Sally.

Tamsin looked up and straight into her laptop and smiled, "Hell!" she replied. "We have lost most of our nursing staff to the Covid wards and of those remaining, some are sick while others have to stay at home to look after their children." It wasn't a moan, just a statement of fact. "But," she added, "this is what we signed up to". Tamsin was expressing her duty and sacrifice and that morning, as we all looked at our screens, God honoured her.

The most ordinary and noblest man in the Bible

Honour played a large part in the Eastern culture where Saju was born and raised. Honour, whether that means authority and leadership, money, eating or styles of humour, are seen not individually but collectively. Deeds and actions are judged as to whether they brought honour or shame on the family or the neighbourhood. If Saju did something wrong then his mother would scold him with something along the lines of, "Shame on you. What will the neighbours say?" Conversely if he did what was right, it would bring honour to the family and neighbourhood and there would be much admiration in his mother's eyes. Family honour played a vital part in his childhood.

With this background, Saju can visualise the prevailing culture in Bible times. Understanding the importance of this culture might help in understanding the nobility of an ordinary yet remarkable man in the Bible. It will also help to understand the pain and cost that this noble man suffered. Though underrated, he is deserving of great honour. His name was Joseph. He lived in a backwater town called Nazareth and earned his living as a carpenter. However, God called him to be the step-father of Jesus, born of Mary. This was God in the world who was to be the saviour of all people.

Nowadays Joseph seems totally overshadowed by the veneration given to Mary, his wife, yet Joseph is the epitome of everything honourable and noble. He is a good person in the Bible to think about if confronted and worried about difficult decisions.

Mary, his espoused but not yet married wife, was pregnant – and it wasn't him! He didn't realise that the child was of the Holy Spirit and that the child's father was God. He most likely would have felt angry and betrayed but, when he got all that out of his system, he would have been left with the worry of what to do. If he didn't understand Mary's pregnancy, his community in a little town like Nazareth, certainly would not understand. The family background in which Saju was raised would have prevailed then – very strongly. Mary would bring shame, on not just the family, but also on the whole community. What a dilemma! The struggle in this young man is only too clear to see behind the words in Matthew 1:19. "Because Joseph her husband was a righteous man and did not want to expose her to public disgrace, he had in mind to divorce her quietly," In a word – Joseph was worried.

This is where the nobility of this young man steps in, for Joseph owed a greater duty and sacrifice to God and so started a series of "God-to-Joseph dreams" which were vital for the birth, protection and care of the infant Jesus. Only a noble man with a great sense of duty and sacrifice could have achieved this. God knew this. That is why he chose Joseph. Four times God spoke to Joseph in a dream and four times Joseph got up and, in humility, obeyed immediately without fully understanding God's direction. First, he was told that, in spite of appearances, he was not to be afraid to take Mary as his wife. Second, Jesus was born into "the house and line of David (Luke 2:4)" but Joseph was directed to get out of Bethlehem asap, without any inkling or idea that Herod's soldiers would shortly come to kill babies under the age of two. Third, now in Egypt and perhaps making his living, he was told to return to Israel and fourth, while on his way back, probably to Bethlehem, he was directed not to settle in Judea as it was too dangerous but to settle in Galilee. So he took his family back to Mary's home town of Nazareth. Each direction was vital for the survival and upbringing of Jesus. His actions honoured God that in turn bought honour to his family that we celebrate each year, particularly at Christmas. Truly, this noble man is one of the best to think about.

Joseph was noble but he showed another God characteristic as well. Joseph was not only noble, but he was also just. "Because Joseph was a righteous man..." The example of Joseph leads from thinking about whatever is noble to the next God characteristic – thinking about whatever is right or just.

Prayer: *Thank you that you are an honourable and noble God and that you love our worship honouring your Holy name. We give you thanks for medical staff and pray for their protection as they continue their work. Lord may our worried minds transcend out of worry as we think and pray for them together with carers and patients in care homes, for teachers and children in schools, and for shop staff and customers.*

Questions you might like to consider:

- Where do you see the virtue of being noble in your world?
- What are your reflections on how honour is understood in different cultures?
- Is there someone that you know who is honourable and noble? Can you see this into your own life? Do you see where honour can change the community where you live and bring peace?
- What thoughts would you include if you wrote this chapter on whatever is honourable or noble?

CHAPTER SIX

THINKING ABOUT
WHAT IS JUST

I was hungry and you gave me something to eat.
Matthew 25:35

The Pool of Siloam was located outside Old Jerusalem's city walls but nobody knew exactly where it was. In 2004 workmen, repairing a large water pipe, came across steps leading down so archaeologists were called in. Was this the pool of Siloam that features in John 5:1–15?

Jesus was in Jerusalem for the Feast of the Jews. On the Sabbath, he went to the pool by the sheep gate known as the Pool of Siloam. Gathered around the pool were the disabled, the lame and the paralysed. Legend had it that when the waters stirred, it's magical properties would heal the first one who managed to get into the pool.

An invalid for 38 years was at the Pool of Siloam. Jesus found him and asked him if he wanted to be well. The invalid explained that he needed someone to help him because he could never get into the pool fast enough after the water stirred as someone else always got there first. So Jesus healed him and the man stood, Jesus told him to pick up his mat and walk out of that place of sickness and injustice. So in the end he didn't need the pool. What he needed was Jesus. The lack of justice continued as the Jews then accused the man of breaking the rules of the Sabbath. Apparently, the offence was that the man should not have been carrying his mat. Oh you naughty, naughty boy! If you had stayed there sitting on your mat for the rest of the day, you would not have broken the law. I know this looks incredulous through my twenty-first century western eyes but, isn't this taking rules a little too far? It was as if these people somehow resented this man's release from his 38 year-long hell. That is where he was and that is where he should have stayed. Fortunately, that is where Jesus was as well. If anybody wanted to find Jesus, he would frequently be amongst the sick and those imprisoned in the darkness of their souls.

Cardboard city

Who do you think said this? "God is in the slums, in the cardboard boxes where the poor play house. God is in the silence of a mother who has infected her child with a virus that will end both of their lives. God is in the cries heard under the rubble of war. God is in the debris of wasted opportunity and lives, and God is with us if we are with them". Any thoughts? Some Archbishop maybe? Or perhaps it was the Pope? The answer might be a surprise.

The answer is – Bono! Yes, the lead vocalist and lyric writer of the rock band U2. President George W. Bush invited Bono to speak at the 54th National Prayer Breakfast at the White House. Bono clearly thought a lot about what is right and just and he didn't pull any punches when it came to expressing those thoughts. Saju is a great fan of Bono! In fact, if anything can get Saju angry, it's when he comes across injustice. I have seen the frustration on his face when he asks Christians. "What kind of faith do we profess if it is not based on human justice?"

Humankind might ignore the cries of the poor. A friend of mine returned from a trip abroad and told me that the country that he had been visiting demanded that prospective patients put up a substantial deposit, way beyond the means of the poor, before they can have medical treatment in a hospital. Yet God is a just God. He hates the injustice that prevents the poor selling their products while the world sings the virtues of a free market. He hates injustice that emanates from racial prejudice, gender prejudice, age prejudice or any other prejudice. Saju, zooming with me about whatever is just, was in full cry, "The parameters of our just God are not written either by the left or by the right wings of politics. Our God is a God not only of Abraham, Isaac and Jacob. Our God is the God of the least and the lost and the last".

This brings up an uncomfortable question. What are my thoughts on this? I can relate to domestic injustice the sort that Clement and Co at the church at Philippi faced with the ladies at war with each other. I can relate and recall the justice that I meted out to my children as they were growing up from infancy. I remember quietly dealing, away from PR interference, with the rarity of disputes at work arising between members of my staff. I remember only too well trying to smooth out the moans and groans that I had while leading the church. However, these are a far cry from "God is in the slums". Can I honestly say that I am anywhere near the "slums" where God is? The question came home to roost while I was looking at a sculptured frieze at the front of Notre Dame Cathedral, Paris.

The cathedral of Notre Dame, Paris (before the fire)

I was standing outside Notre Dame with a group of people I didn't know and looking at the great west elevation with its porticos, statues, carvings and towers. Along with the others in the group, our attention was being drawn to a sculptured frieze above one of the great doors. "Look," said the walking tour guide, "that frieze represents the last judgment. In the middle seated on a throne is Jesus judging the world. To his right of the throne is a line of people going to heaven. To the left of the throne is a line of people going to hell." All seemed to recognise what the frieze meant.

Then he asked, "Who are in the line going to heaven?" Nearly everybody in the group put their hands up. "Oh yes," they said, "we are in that line". The tour guide looked pleased. "Is there anyone here in the group leading to the other place?" he challenged laughing.

Nervously I put my hand up, "Yes, I should be in that group".

The tour operator looked astonished. He had probably run this little routine many times before. I suddenly felt the eyes of everybody looking at me.

I wondered for a long time what had made me put my hand up then. I knew assuredly as a child of God that my home was in heaven because Jesus had carried my sins and shortcomings on the cross. I wondered what the qualities were of those on the right side of the throne of Jesus and how they differed from those on the left. Was it because they were good people? Was it because that, in spite of having occasional slip ups, they weren't as bad as others? No – the basis of Jesus' judgment came down to whether or not they had fed the hungry and thirsty. I put my hand up because I suddenly became aware of my shortcoming.

The frieze on the front elevation of Notre Dame Cathedral is a representation of the Parable of the Sheep and Goats to be found in Matthew 25. The parable tells us that judgment will be passed on all nations, both the righteous (sheep) and the unrighteous (goats). All are judged on whether they fed the hungry and thirsty; or invited the stranger into their presence; or provided clothing to the destitute; or supported the sick or visited those in prison. This is where Jesus is and those ignoring these needs will be judged to be goats and everlastingly separated from the God of justice.

Uncomfortably I realised that I was a "goat" if ever there was one! How much time do I give to helping with the hungry and thirsty? Yet more recently I have come to realise that my interpretation of Jesus parable about the sheep and the goats might be considered in a slightly different way. "All the nations will be gathered before him," is written in Matthew 25:32. This is about communities. What does our community do to feed the hungry and thirsty? This in no way lets me, or any of us, off the hook. It asks all of us, "What are we doing within our community do help the hungry and thirsty. Are we in a community of sheep or are we a community of goats?" Where do we start within our relatively wealthy nation? Here is a little allegory that might give us a steer.

A father and son set out for a walk one morning across a nearby beach. As they walked, they found hundreds of washed up starfish covering the beach. There had been a storm in the night and the waves had stranded the poor creatures on the shore.

"None of them will live," said the father, "they will all die".

The boy looked at his dad and then solemnly picked up one of the starfish and threw it with all his might back into the sea. "Well," said the boy, "there is one that will live". Perhaps we might think of stories we have heard or been involved in where "starfish" have been thrown back into the sea.

Feeding the hungry and thirsty – Rita

In 1944, the year I was born, the Soviet Union occupied the little Balkan country of Latvia. A family – father, mother and their daughter fled into Germany from the Soviet tanks. I remember my mother explaining to me what a refugee was. My father was an avid Rotarian and it was through the community of the Rotary Club that my parents "adopted" this Latvian family. I remember seeing them packing parcels of food up ready to be sent to the refugee camp where this family now resided. In turn, the refugee family would send back little gifts of needlework. Rita, their daughter, was a little older than me became a very adept seamstress even as a little girl. Some 10 years later, the Rotary Club afforded the journey for Rita to come to England. I remember her well. She was pretty and blond while I was a very awkward spotty teenager. She was all over me and I did not know what to make of it but I think she was showering her gratitude for what the community had done for her and her family. Later my parents acquired a beautiful hand carved figure of a Latvian shepherdess. I still have it. It exudes serenity and peace and occupies pride-of-place in our sitting room.

What struck me is that my parents were not acting alone. They were part of a club of other members also helping refugees from Latvia. My parents were able to assist a family through the community they lived in. Here are other more up to date examples of people feeding the hungry and thirsty with the help of community.

Feeding the hungry and thirsty – Jan

Jan felt a familiar nudge from God who wanted her to do something. At that time, she was becoming aware that she wanted to reach out to the needy and was attracted initially to organising some sort of aid to the Yemen. So, heart in mouth, she rang UNICEF. She really did not know whether she would get any response from such a huge organisation but to her surprise, she received a very accommodating call the next day. It was explained that providing aid to the Yemen could prove tricky but they really needed help with supplies to the huge and vastly overcrowded refugee camp in Lesbos, a Greek island. What they wanted was sleeping bags, hand wash and toiletries. Clothes were on the list too. The reaction to her plea to the community was dynamic. Around 550 sleeping bags were amassed. Her garage was crammed. Eventually it took two lorry loads of the sleeping bags, thousands of toiletries and a huge collection of clothes for all ages. In addition, over £5,000 was raised which was used to purchase at phenomenal discounts. She wondered, "The supplies were so much it seemed it was multiplying like five loaves and two fishes". Some may recall the news of the terrible fire in the Lesbos camp. However, the shipment went out after the fire and therefore was not lost. Jan humbly won't take any credit. As far as she was concerned, this is the work of God, the God of Justice. Yet she experienced opposition to what she was doing... incredible... surprised?

Jan was part of our church and had a very heightened sense of the need for justice. Through her prompting, the community responded. They really responded! My third example is of a community who were, at first, reluctant to respond.

Feeding the hungry and thirsty – a former prisoner

Saju' told me of a man he knew who had served a prison sentence. After his release, he developed a concern particularly for people who had served time in prison and were adjusting back to life outside. So he opened a food club which provided regular meals. He reached out to the hungry and thirsty. Regrettably, the church did not get involved. When Saju found out he was amazed. Surely, the project was just the sort of thing that the church should get involved in. The reason for the community's reluctance was eventually revealed. People in the church were well-meaning but they were also scared. Fear was stopping them entering an environment with those sort of people. After a bit of cajoling (being cajoled by Saju is not to be relished!) they overcame their fear and began to see with their own eyes how people were being empowered to live in their own right and not always be on the receiving end.

The next example is really quite sad. This is where the community did not respond and it was left to a couple to give help where it was needed.

Feeding the hungry and thirsty – Mike and Fray

Mike and Fray were in A&E. The police arrived and dumped a man at the door. He was only semi-conscious and had to be lifted into a chair by two bystanders – while clearly in an alcohol-induced dream and mumbling "No! You're all trying to kill me." Fast forward a few hours and the man was back to a reasonable level of sobriety and released into the waiting room. Unable to find his possessions and missing his shoes, he stood in the waiting room filled with people pleading for some change to buy a drink from the vending machines. Everyone hid their faces and tried to ignore him. After a while with no help coming, Mike got up and went over to the man. He offered to buy something for him, finding out what he wanted and then buying him two bottles of Fanta from the vending machine. The man wanted to repay Mike but was assured that no payment was necessary. So instead, the man offered a prayer. He put his hands together, looked up and asked for blessings for the young couple – "in the name of the Father, Son, and the Holy Ghost," he said recalling something learned long ago. Fray told him that when he first arrived she was praying for him too. He was thankful for the prayer – and the refreshment.

Clothing the destitute – Julia and George

History has a way of repeating itself. I started this compendium of communities helping the destitute with a story beginning in 1944 with the Soviet invasion of Latvia. Then in 2022, just 76 years later it seems to have happened all over again with the Russian invasion of Ukraine. As with all terrible invasions of countries resulting in war, people flee or are driven out from their homes, their towns and cities. A young Ukrainian woman and her son had managed to get out, refugees with nothing but the clothes in which they stood. Exhausted and traumatised they had found their way to England and had been housed with a Christian family. Quickly the host family realised that this Ukrainian mother and son needed everything to help them find their dignity, and, in some measure, their lives. Clothing was identified as the prime need.

And so the host family put out a call to local friends asking for clothing. The call began a network of response. For example, a couple living nearby received the call via a text message. The urgency was obvious. They put off what they had planned for the evening and drove to the local shopping centre. There they purchased a full set of clothes for both mother and son, dropping the much needed clothes off at an agreed point. The network had been fruitful and many people had contributed. The Ukrainian mother and son were overwhelmed by the generosity and kindness that had been shown to them in the gifts of much needed clothing.

Even in the darkest and most foul of times, the light of God shines. God, who is love, cares deeply for each one of us. His love may be realised in the small but significant acts of kindness of his people.

"I tell you the truth (said Jesus) whatever you did for one of the least of these brothers and sisters of mine, you did for me". Matthew 25:40

The rest of my fellow workers

Thinking about whatever is right or just is daunting if we think of it as a solitary individual. Clement didn't have to sort out the rights and wrongs of the problem before him on his own. He was there with "the rest of my fellow workers".

God never intends for us to face the enormity of injustice in the world individually. It would overwhelm. I find comfort in this but also responsibility. I may not be a front line worker dealing with injustice but I can provide support of some kind. Community is key here. Do we, in our community, respond to God's calling to find him in the slums? Or do we, in our community, hide our face from the poverty around us? Will we be judged by the God of justice to be sheep or goats?

Something else dawned in my thoughts. These blessed souls were serving God while they were serving the lost. Each example displayed a contentment in what they were doing. I was going to find out just how important this was if I was going to understand what Paul meant when he wrote, "I have learned the secret of contentment in any and every situation" (4:12).

Prayer: *Lord, people flocked to you asking for mercy and healing. We come to you asking for forgiveness. We who have much have often failed to give to those who have little. We know how much this grieves you. Send your Holy Spirit on people in the country suffering at this time, to reach out to others whose want is greater than ours. Then Lord direct our minds to think on these things.*

Questions you might like to consider

The fourth mark of mission in the Anglican church is as follows, "To seek to transform unjust structures of society, to challenge violence of every kind and to pursue peace and reconciliation". How do you consider your church measures up to this mark of mission?

What does it mean for the church to recover its prophetic edge, voice and action?

What drives you to seek justice in this world or conversely what drives you away?

Can you see where the presence of God can help you with some aspect of what is just and what is right?

What thoughts would you include if you wrote this chapter on whatever is just or right?

CHAPTER SEVEN

THINKING ABOUT
WHATEVER IS PURE

Blessed are the pure in heart for they shall see God.
Matthew 5:8

Thinking about whatever is pure – you must be joking!

You may recall from chapter three that this is what I wrote in my daybook at the outset of my deliberations about this passage. I was, initially, very reluctant even to consider writing this book and uppermost in my mind was making sense of thinking whatever is pure in order to transcend worry. God knew that I needed help and this started the day that I sat down to think about whatever is pure with Saju.

"Seeking to be pure and blameless from a moral point of view, will provide us all with a struggle – almost certainly a hopeless struggle". This was one of the first comments that I wrote down from what he said and with it, I felt a great sense of relief, but relief was quickly followed by stupefaction.

"I want us to think about Dorian Gray," he said

"You mean the chap who had his portrait painted?" I replied, trying to keep up.

"The very same."

And so we began to think about a strange story written by Oscar Wilde about a young man who was anything but pure.

Dorian Gray

An artist painted a portrait of Dorian Gray who was a beautiful young man, but with a hedonistic heart. The portrait was initially admired for its beauty but was put in the attic and forgotten whilst the young man continued with his corrupt life. Dorian continued to look beautiful but unknown to him and everyone else the portrait in the attic began to display sores, scars and blemishes. Years later, Dorian, still beautiful, re-discovered the portrait now ugly, gross and distorted. Flying into a rage, he killed the artist and slashed the portrait. Suddenly Dorian looked beautiful no more. His features took on the ugliness of the portrait. All appearances were gone. He was now seen for what he really was.

This is a very brief resume of a story holding many lessons. Saju was bringing home to me that the artist represented God whilst we represented the picture. The artist painted a portrait that was beautiful just as God created humankind in his own image and it was good.

"I am fearfully and wonderfully made," wrote King David in Psalm 139:14 but, regrettably, lives become corrupted. This can result in a constant and worrying struggle of presenting ourselves with what we want others to see while at the same time covering up the real "us" that lies in the attic of the soul. Dorian's story illustrates that, when confronted with human corruption, the reaction can be to "kill the artist" as we have seen in Chapter 4 when thinking about whatever is true. There is no redemption in the story of Dorian Gray – no way back. It is the tragic story of life and death. Yet God has created a way back. The cross re-defines the story. Jesus is pure yet became "the picture" bearing humankind's ugliness and despair upon himself. This was a price to be paid and Jesus paid it. At the cross, Jesus took on himself our sin, all the sores and scars that we have created in our life leaving us pure in God's eyes.

Suddenly Saju became animated, "How can a soul, though invisible, be tarnished and therefore what can wash away my sins? – nothing but the blood of Jesus," he cried. "Jesus is beautiful and pure. He is God in the world hanging on the cross, covered in the sores and scabs of our sin. The worried soul asks God to be free of sin and impurities and the wish is granted. The attic of the soul is cleared out and the contents destroyed. This is God's work achieved by the cross. He died hideously but his last words were "It is finished" – his task was completed. God's purity is manifested in this work of completion. The worried soul can now walk free, pure in God's eyes. This is what it means to be saved by the blood of Christ".

As I sat scribbling down what Saju was saying, I realised that thinking about what Jesus completed on the cross is pure. However, Saju bought home to me something else that morning. Purity also lies in all tasks completed by men and women to spread the work of Jesus and the cross. Thinking about whatever is pure began to open up. I could expand my thinking to a venture undertaken and completed by a man or woman. I asked Saju to suggest an example of someone the next time we met and, at the same time, I would also think of an example. Suitable examples were boundless! So you might imagine my surprise when we both came up with exactly the same illustration! It was not anything from our ministries, or anything we had heard from others. Neither did we come up with an example from the Bible. What we both came up with was the story of how an amazing piece of music was composed.

We both listen to this oratorio and I have sung in it. It told the story of the cross and resurrection. It's Handel's 'Messiah'

George Frideric Handel and 'Messiah'

In 1743, King George II attended the London premier of the great oratorio. As tradition will have it, King George, sitting in the audience and listening to the beauty of the music, got completely carried away and stood up during the "Alleluia Chorus". Because the King was standing, everybody else had to stand as well. Even today, when the oratorio is performed, the audience honours the excellence of the music by standing at the "Alleluia Chorus". But George Frideric Handel, court composer to the King, knew that there was something pure behind his 'Messiah'.

Handel did not have an easy life. At times, he faced debt and prison. Like other great composers, his genius was attacked throughout his life and particularly by the church. The problem the church had with Handel's oratorios, like Esther and Samson, was that they were Biblical dramas often played in secular settings rather than in church buildings.

Although born German, Handel spent much of his life in the courts of the Hanoverian Kings George I and George II. Handel was given a libretto comprising a compilation of Biblical prophecy and began composing 'Messiah'. Something then happened in his life as he encountered God in a way that he had never experienced before. He literally went into his room in his small house in London, started composing, and emerged less than four weeks later with the masterpiece completed. Morning, noon and night – this was a time of intense composition and reflection during which he was captivated by God and the purity of what God had done through Jesus – The Messiah, God in the world. The oratorio is in three parts. Part one was finished in six days. Part two took longer – nine days. Part three took a further six days. It was shortly after, that his servant came into his room and found a tearful Handel crying, "I think I did see all heaven before me and the great God himself". Through tears and emotion, he saw the pure beauty of God. The work was completed two days later.

One last thing to know about this masterpiece. A typical performance lasts two-and-a-half to three hours. A full performance would last longer but conductors most frequently cut out some of the oratorio as it is often considered too long for today's audience. Yet God inspired Handel to complete this enormous act of worship in 24 days!

"It is finished," shouted Jesus on the cross taking our sin upon himself once-and-for-all. Surely Handel must have felt the same – "it is finished" – as he staggered out of that small room in London having completed a great piece of music about the cross, after an intense period of creativity of 24 days. Thinking about "Messiah" is to think about whatever is pure.

Sister Wendy Beckett

Saju, having "pinched" my example, left me having to think of another example of whatever is pure. My mind strayed a little as I reasoned, "On the cross, Jesus also said 'Father, into your hands I commit my spirit' (Luke 23:46). Surely, thinking on this would also be thinking about whatever is pure". So I began to think of someone who I had come across who committed their lives wholly and entirely to God. I had many examples, but I have always been intrigued by a Roman Catholic nun who became a television personality. Sister Wendy Beckett.

There was something beautiful and pure about Sister Wendy Beckett. She was not beautiful in the conventional sense.

Her beauty shone from the grace that was within. She became a very unusual TV star in the 1990s. Televised both in the UK and USA, Sister Wendy bought us little gems as she stood before various paintings and explained what they were and what they represented. She became hugely popular, drawing very substantial viewing figures. Apparently, the production team never had to do more than one take. "Action" was called, the cameras rolled, and Sister Wendy would talk perfectly on the matter in hand with no notes or cues. She was both very knowledgeable but she presented it all with such gentleness. Sister Wendy saw God clearly when she wrote, "Scripture tells us that one of the great joys on entering heaven will be that God will call us by our name. In fact God is the only one who really knows our name because he is the only one who knows us absolutely."

She said that her love for art was a way of loving God, yet first and foremost, her heart was devoted to prayer. She eventually ended her TV days and devoted herself completely to the prayer life that God had ordained for her to do. She wrote, "Prayer is never an escape but the opposite, an exposure". Sister Wendy inspired me. I thank God that she was lent to our world to delight so many with her love and interpretation of art. She died doing what God called her to do – committing her spirit to prayer.

So, I am able to think of whatever is pure through someone who has composed a piece of music centred on the cross of Jesus. I am able to think of whatever is pure through a person's commitment to God through her love of art and her quiet devotion to prayer. Nevertheless, we cannot all be George Frideric Handel, nor can we be Sister Wendy Beckett. What about Mr and Mrs Ordinary? I thought of a Bible story in Luke chapter 10 when Jesus sent out disciples to go into towns that he was intending to visit. Their job was to herald the coming of the saviour of the world.

Purity in service

Jesus gathered 72 disciples together with the objective of sending them into the community in pairs. I imagined them all lined up before him ready with both anticipation and uncertainty with Jesus looking at all of them and making sure that they understood the cost of the task that lay before them. The briefing went something like this:

> "Right everybody. I want you to think about your mission like a farmer going to harvest a field. The harvest is plentiful but there are not many of you and it will not be a cakewalk. You are going to be like lambs among wolves. Now gather round and listen very carefully to my instructions. When you reach a town, find a house to stay in and the first thing you do is bless the house with God's peace. If you are accepted then that is very good. Stay there. Heal the sick. Do not look for anything better. If you are not accepted in a town, then waste no time with it. The fate of that town will be worse than what happened to Sodom. (Sodom was destroyed by a storm of burning sulphur raining down from the sky) (Taken from Luke 10:1–12).

There is no doubt in the mind of the gospel writer, Jesus told it the way it was. He did not pull any punches. The task before the 72 was a difficult one and there was no obvious outcome here. The previous attempt to send the 12 disciples into the community had resulted in dismal failure (Luke 9). These were men whose names are known and, in the case of Peter, James, John, Andrew, Philip, Nathanael, Matthew and Thomas, we know a little more than just their names. Now Jesus gathers six times the number and we do not know the identity of any of them. These were 72 totally unsung heroes. This exercise would be a trial but they came through! By faith, two by two went out and two by two they came back with wonderful stories to tell and they were full of it!

It had been a complete success, "Lord even the demons submit to us" (Luke 10:17).

The nobodies had completed their job and God was applauding. We read that Jesus was, "full of joy through the Holy Spirit" (Luke 10:21). Pure joy! Just imagine the seventy-two buzzing around him in great excitement as they relayed their stories while Jesus was all smiles and laughter – over the moon with delight.

Seventy-two ordinary people yet they went out and heralded Jesus. Seventy-two ordinary people – that is about the size of an ordinary church facing a difficult task of going into the community without an obvious outcome. Yet some go through the trial and come back with wonderful stories. Only a few will reach the headlines but their acts are there for us to think about.

I think of a couple who lived on a boat yet turned up each week in church to pray with us, work with us and to sing in the music group that led our worship. They eventually decided to buy another boat – a canal boat and as far as I know, are sailing happily around the waterways of England, their work with us having been completed.

I think of a wonderful lady who is the same age as I am and who I call my sister. She worked constantly and consistently for our church as Church Secretary and Electoral Role Officer until she retired from the positions. Unsung except by those who think about what she did over those years holding the administration of our church together as we set about proclaiming the cross.

I think about completing my own work as a church leader, leaving the work to continue in the hands of younger people. After I stepped down. I took time out so that they could find their legs without me. When Sally and I returned, I was moved to find out how much they missed me, but I know that I would never have coped as leader with the challenges that Covid later threw up before them. They bought the church through those difficult days and gradually the church is returning to what it was and even better. I completed my work and others took on the mantle of proclaiming Jesus to our community. Thinking about this humble unacclaimed work is thinking about whatever is pure.

Heart

We have now reached the half-way point in our "Whatever's". We have considered whatever is true, noble, and just and we are about to consider whatever is lovely, admirable – excellent and praiseworthy. Thinking about whatever is pure is at the heart of our thinking. Somehow, everything else seems to revolve around this. To think about whatever is pure is to think about the cross of Jesus and I have come to understand from my initial reticence that thinking about whatever is pure takes us from the cross to proclaiming Jesus to our communities.

There is something rather lovely about what Jesus said about pure. He went up a mountain that he used as a pulpit to preach his most famous sermon – the Sermon on the Mount. It started with blessings that included, "Blessed are the pure in heart for they shall see God (Matthew 5:8). What a wonderful promise! God is pure. God is also love. Where love is, God is there – at the heart. That is lovely and this is what we are going to consider next – whatever is lovely.

Prayer: *Lord, we pray that you will sustain all those that you have given a task to do. Send them others who can encourage especially when the going gets tough. Let all working for you know that they have a purity that only God is and only God can give.*

Questions you might like to consider:

- What is the difference between purity and perfection?
- How is Jesus pure?
- Is there someone that you know who is pure in heart? Can you put this into practice for yourself?
- What thoughts would you include if you wrote this chapter on whatever is pure?

CHAPTER EIGHT

THINKING ABOUT WHATEVER IS LOVELY

How lovely is your dwelling place,
O Lord Almighty, my soul yearns even faints
for the courts of the Lord, my heart and flesh
cry out for the living God.
Psalm 84:1–2

There was a ring at the door. It was Sally. "Come on," she said, "we are going for a walk". So we set off across a local beauty spot commonly known as "The Banks". At first, we were silent as we walked side-by-side and then she said, "Let's think about things that are lovely".

I now knew why this lovely lady had rung my bell. I was down. I was worried to the point of despair and she knew it. She always knew. Nobody else could have asked me to think about whatever was lovely that day because I really, really did not want to think about ANYTHING – least of all anything lovely. So, in obedience to her wishes, I began to think and by the time we had crossed the first "bank" I was making headway – albeit falteringly. By the time we turned back for home, I was in full flow. We said goodbye outside where I was living. As I looked at her face, I realised that I loved this lovely person never realising that many years later we would be married.

Thinking about whatever is lovely is sometimes a good place to start when we want to replace worry and transcend beyond it. Yet surprisingly I find that it is the last place I want to start particularly when I am worried. To put it bluntly – I might just not be in the mood. I have found that there are times when I need the help of a good friend to think about whatever is lovely. And then... well then, it can just pour out! There is much that is lovely to fill worried lives. Family, loved ones, friends – lovely people, lovely stories about lovely people, lovely Bible stories – lovely places to visit, views and waterfalls – oh I just love waterfalls! The choice is "wide, wide as the ocean" as we used to sing when I was very much younger. "Wide, wide as the ocean... is my saviour's love for me"

So, I am going to begin my thoughts at a good place to start. A story from the Bible – one that I consider to be the loveliest of all.

A Bible story that is lovely

When tragedy strikes it seems to come in fork loads – or so it seemed to the elderly woman as she started her journey with her belongings in a small handcart and a stick in her hand. Behind her followed two young women. One of the girls kept pace with the old woman, the other was falling behind as if she were tiring. They had not gone far when the old woman stopped and turned.

"Listen this isn't right – you following me. I am returning to my own country, to my home town of Bethlehem. Go back. You stay in Moab. Find other husbands."

"No, no," they both replied. "We are coming with you."

Hearing this, the elderly woman turned up the pressure. "What on earth do you want to come with me for? My husband is dead. My sons – your husbands – have both died. Can I provide more sons for you to marry? For goodness sake, see sense and go back." And with that she trudged on leaving the girls standing on the road. They looked at each other knowing what the other was thinking. They hugged and Orpah, the elder girl, started back. Ruth, the younger watched her go then turned and raced after Naomi, her mother-in-law.

Naomi heard running feet behind her. She did not turn to look but became aware that Ruth had dropped in beside her. Naomi stopped, bewildered and frustrated:

"Look, didn't I tell you..."

"Hush mother. Do not urge me to turn back from you. Where you go, I will go, and where you stay, I will stay. Your people will be my people and your God will be my God. Where you die, I will die and there I will be buried" (Ruth 1:16-17).

Naomi was looking at the loveliest and most determined face she had ever seen. Indeed, it remains one of the loveliest things ever said by one person to another in the Bible or anywhere. The two women walked on together to their destiny in Bethlehem. It was there, as the story unfolds, that Naomi helped Ruth find a husband. Ruth married Boaz and gave birth to a son and later became great-grandmother to the great King David. Naomi found a dwelling place with her new family (You can read this beautiful story in the book of Ruth).

What they did not know is that many years later a young couple also set out on a long walk to Bethlehem. The difficulty that they endured was even worse because the young girl was heavily pregnant. Shortly after their arrival in Bethlehem, she gave birth to the Saviour of the World – God with us – and they called him Jesus in accordance with God's instructions. Matthew's gospel starts with a genealogy leading up to that birth. Ruth is one of the five women listed.

* * * *

When I left school, I was lonely. I tried a number of things but it was not until a friend invited me to church that I began to see a way out of loneliness. The church was running a house party for the late teens and early twenties. I did not know any of the thirty or forty young people going to the house party but I was encouraged by two young men who offered to give me a lift. I decided to take a chance and go. The two young men sat in the front seat of the car and talked avidly together while I sat silently in the back. The conversation between the two was about the good-humoured mischief they were planning with others in their group whilst keeping one-step ahead of David, the man running the house party. The closer we got to our destination, the more apprehensive I became. Eventually I blurted out from the back seat, "Look chaps, when we get there, you go off and join your friends and point me at David. I'll be alright".

The two young men in the front seat stopped talking and there was a silence for a moment. Then the one not driving turned and said, "Look John, you are with us and you are going to be part of our group and if anybody says otherwise, we are all going home". It was one of the loveliest things that has ever had said to me. A lonely young man had found his dwelling place.

Thinking about whatever is lovely may create moments that simply takes the breath away. The above stories hold that kind of moment. Nevertheless, there is something much more permanent about these stories than just a fleeting moment of loveliness. Naomi was accepted by Ruth and she went on to be part of a family that would support her. In that process, she found God's dwelling place and a new family. Hundreds of years later, I was accepted by two young strangers and went on to become part a church family that would lead me toward a long ministry as a lay leader and a purpose in life.

People are lovely

As I have become older, I have come to see the loveliness of God in people. This gives me great joy but also a sense of sadness. Sadness because loveliness is not, in my view, the prerogative of Christians. What a shame! It is sad because Christians should be known for their loveliness or their love for one another (see John 13:35) Nevertheless, it is a joy to see lovely God-characteristics ingrained in people even though they might not believe in God. Since walking with Saju down the Champs Elysees, Paris in chapter 1, life has not been kind to me and my mobility has suffered. I am just amazed how people respond so quickly if they see me struggling to get up or climb a steep step. Perhaps this was in the mind of Thomas Merton, monk, writer, theologian and social activist, when he wrote:

> "I have the immense joy of being [human], a member of a race in which God became incarnate. As if the sorrows and stupidities of the human condition could overwhelm me, now I realize what we all are. And if only everybody could realise this! But it cannot be explained. There is no way of telling people that they are all walking around shining like the sun!"

I see that "sun" as God in people even if they do not recognise it themselves. I felt the warmth of that "sun" when Sally and I were visiting one of those houses you pay money to visit. It was not a big house but to get our money's worth we would need to climb to the first floor. That meant stairs! But I was determined as the risers didn't look too steep. Visiting was controlled.

We booked a time slot and arrived along with others who had booked that same slot and then, having gathered we went from one room to the next. There were a lot of artefacts in the rooms, so there was a volunteer on hand in each room both to protect and inform. Our tour started and went into the first room. "Welcome!" said the volunteer and then seeing me added "Would you like to sit down?" I told her that I would prefer to stand. The group progressed to the second room and another volunteer said to me, "Would you like to sit down?" I gave her the same response. The group reached the third room and again I got, "Would you like to sit down?" The group began to laugh. Then came the stairs. The group mounted the steps and I went last. Half way up I started to breathe heavily but I wasn't going to be beaten. I reached the dog-leg – two more stairs and I was there! I arrived upstairs at the fourth room breathing hard. There was another volunteer in the room. By now, everyone was hushed in anticipation waiting, knowing what would come. "Do you want to sit down?" she asked – "NO I DON'T WANNA SIT DOWN!!" The group convulsed. It was now time to go down the stairs. The group descended and I followed. Half way down I saw a volunteer standing at the bottom. She was young and, let us just say she was amply built. There she stood, arms outstretched, "Come on John you can make it. If you fall I will catch you and you will have a squidgy landing!" Lovely people. Lovely people who have God's innate loveliness born within them. The importance of those lovely moments cannot be underestimated.

> How lovely is an unworried face
> full of beauty, full of grace
> The voice of an unworried mother
> The sweet voice of a sister or brother
> Urging us on to make us sing
> encouraging and comforting
> I pray my face is worry free
> a glowing sun for all to see

A lovely story

Saju needed time out. Those who cared for his work as a priest advised a sabbatical. Saju grasped the opportunity with both hands and decided to use the opportunity to head for the world! One location was the furthermost location from our islands of Great Britain – New Zealand.

"Are you going right down to the bottom of South Island?" I asked him one day before he left "Why don't you try getting to Milford Sound. I have not been myself but I gather it is quite amazing. However," I then added casually "I think that the weather is pretty lousy most of the time". Little did I know that Saju lapped up every word.

Milford Sound is a spectacular fjord situated toward the southern extremity of South Island. It is one of the most visually stunning locations in the world, albeit it is rarely open to clear blue skies. There are no motorways in that part of South Island and it took four hours for Saju to drive from where he was staying. He marvelled at what he saw, sights that will forever be remembered. However, the weather began to worsen and he realised that he had to return to the car. The road was becoming waterlogged and it looked like it was going to flood so there was no turning back. He then came to a halt. The bridge that carried the road ahead had collapsed. He could not go on and he could not go back. He was, well and truly stuck. He could have had a funny moment and freaked, instead, thankfully, he was equipped with both a presence of mind and a charged up mobile. Reaching for the phone, he was told to be prepared to be airlifted out. Alas, Saju is afraid of flying. When younger, he would take any opportunity to get into the air but then, typically of Saju, he started reading all about it and particularly everything that could go wrong in flight. Too much knowledge! Knowing too much made him prone to worry. But worry was replaced with the fascination of the lovely spectacle of a helicopter coming to his rescue out of the gloom and landing on the road. So he videoed the event! After he got home, the church was entertained by his story and video and typically, he rounded the story off with a flourish by announcing to the church, how I had led him into near catastrophe!

Yet there was something even more lovely than the spectacle of the fjord or the sight of the helicopter coming to his rescue. He told me later how all that was eclipsed by the moment he returned home to Katy and his four children, to his people, his church – and even to me!

There is much that I have written and then omitted from this chapter. Thinking about whatever is lovely is like a waterfall. It starts to gush and does not dry up. I want to finish with another Bible story. It is the story of Noah. It is a very familiar and lovely story known by many and told to children. However, I want to concentrate on a less familiar part of it.

God is lovely

What could be more lovely than the sight of an olive leaf? The olive leaf must have been the loveliest thing that Noah had seen for months. Just imagine what it would be like waking up every morning to a scene of unbroken sea. No land, no end in sight, together with the stink that must have greeted them from the menagerie that they had on board! There they floated day after day, endlessly rocking at the mercy of storms. They had survived the devastation but they must have felt loss very keenly thinking about those they knew and loved who had perished in the flood.

Noah's story can be found in Genesis 6–9. Noah was a man who knew God, had faith in God and never gave up hope. He sent out a bird that he had taken into the ark. It was a raven.

It flew around and then flew around some more. Noah did not give up so he tried another bird – a very different bird. This time he chose a dove. The bird came back with an olive leaf in its beak. It meant that the water had receded to the extent that there was dry land sustaining an olive tree somewhere. What joy!

Noah's ark – such an old story only fit to amuse children but it has taken on an up-to-date reality. Perhaps it might remind us of the covid pandemic. We do not have a flood, but we have a virus. We are not locked in a boat, but we have been locked in our homes. Day after day as we mourn the loss of loved ones either through death, or being separated from their presence. We look at the news on the TV each morning and it brings us no hope. The constant media reporting is like the raven that flies round getting nowhere. We yearned to find that "olive leaf" and while we waited, we waited in hope. This very lovely old story usually told to children becomes very relevant to everybody in the 21st century.

Prayer: *Lord you know all about isolation. You suffered the worst isolation of all – the isolation of the cross. Yet in dying for us and rising again, you conquered our isolation from God. Lord, this is the most lovely thing that anyone has ever done. Thank you.*

Perhaps another prayer: *Whatever the darkness we may be in, whatever endless sea we might be on, whatever fog we might be walking in, whatever tunnel we might be crawling through, God grant a moment of loveliness that will lead us to his presence so that we can continue our lives in his dwelling place*

Questions you might like to consider:

* There are pockets of loveliness all around us. Where do you see this in your world?

- What is lovely about the story of Ruth and Naomi?
- Is there a Bible verse that helps you think about what is lovely? Perhaps choose someone in the Bible who is lovely? What in your eyes makes that person lovely.
- Does thinking about "whatever is lovely" help you overcome worry?
- What thoughts would you include if you wrote this chapter on whatever is lovely?

CHAPTER NINE

THINKING ABOUT
WHATEVER IS ADMIRABLE

My joy, my crown
Philippians 4:1

He was standing on the steps of the church on a cold winter morning waiting for me and he was not a happy bunny! I had only recently been licensed as a lay-reader and it was my turn to open the church up for early morning communion and let in the visiting clergyman. We were in an interregnum and we had no vicar. The old vicar had moved on and the new one had yet to come. It had been a long interregnum. We had had a number of false starts but now we had the prospect of a new young vicar who looked promising. We could not wait for him to start. I opened up the church. It was cold and dark. Only about half-a-dozen people turned up. When the service had finished the clergyman, who had conducted Holy Communion, opened up a broadside.

"Are you the Reader here?"

"Well, yes,"

"This church is cold as ice. How can you expect anybody to come if it's so cold?"

"S..s...sorry. The heating system has broken down and we cannot afford to replace it."

"Well, what are you going to do about it then?"

"I... I... will try to get some more heaters."

He then went on to berate me for not having the books he liked available for him to lead the service. It was a difficult experience for a young Reader flung into an Interregnum. I went home crestfallen. This man was not just any old clergyman. This man was the Warden of Readers. He was my boss – the last person that I would want to upset. I looked at my calendar. "Oh Lord", I thought, "he's coming again in four weeks, just after Easter in what we call Low Sunday, and he's going to lead the main Sunday service!"

Four weeks went by. I was determined not to upset him again. I turned up to open the church one hour before the service began, so as to be there before he arrived. No use... he was waiting for me on the church steps. Not a word was uttered between us as I let him in, nor was there any hint of conversation before or during the service. Then, after the service, he purposely drew me aside. I mentally put my crash helmet on and waited for the barrage:

"Mr Bloor I gather you are about to appoint a new vicar."

"Y... yes... that's right."

"He's a very lucky man to be coming to this church (!!! – what??)."

"Er... no... I... I... think you meant to say that w... we are... are very lucky to have him."

"I know what I said, Mr Bloor. He is a very lucky man to have you."

What was this? Surely not... it cannot be? Could this be just the tiniest whisper of admiration? I don't think that he would have ever admitted it but he then went on to explain that the church attendance that day, Low Sunday, was the same as the church attendance on Easter Sunday, the week before. Then he promptly turned on his heel and left. I was dumbfounded. This grumpy Warden of Readers appeared for a moment to admire my little struggling church. Shortly afterwards he stepped down from the office of Warden so I never saw him again. Nevertheless, I shared what he said and it hugely encouraged us.

We appointed the new vicar. He did not disappoint. We were a reduced church that had gone through hard times. We had clung together during those times and we gathered gratefully around him. My Warden of Readers might have been grumpy but he was right. Our new vicar was a lucky man. He could say anything, suggest anything, do anything and we would just roll over and say, "Oh yes please". We loved him and his family and they in turn loved us. We were all content and the church began to fill particularly with younger people. Sally and I are still in touch with them.

Thinking about whatever is admirable has its problems. What we admire is very different and very wide. What we admire is probably lovely and no doubt excellent. I think the story of the grumpy Warden is lovely and so it could fit quite happily in the previous chapter. It matters not. We can think about what is admirable and put it where we want but for the purposes of this chapter, I am going to gather my thoughts on the church and think about the church in respect of whatever is admirable. Paul was certainly lost in admiration for the church he loved.

The church in Philippi

Paul loved the church at Philippi "My joy, my crown!" You can almost see the tears in Paul's eyes as he writes. Even through the problems, he loved and longed for them. He loved the faith of his yokefellow along with Clement and Co. Right at that moment, there was nowhere else that he would rather be. They in turn loved him. They were concerned for him. They were worried about him. Paul wanted to assure them that he was alright, which is one of the reasons why Paul wrote the letter. They did not have to worry. Instead, he tells his beloved church at Philippi to rejoice just as he, Paul, was rejoicing because they had renewed their concern for him (see v10). If we could ask Paul what he most admired, I think that the church at Philippi would be high on the list.

Church, so often criticised, is so wonderful to admire. Here is an example of my admiration of a very different 21st Century church.

A church zooming together

Sally and I have spent several wonderful holidays in a little Spanish town. The first time we went, we saw a shop called "The Anglican Parish Charity Shop". Intrigued, we crossed the road to have a closer look. It was shut! But we noticed a small notice on the door:

> There will be a service
> of Holy Communion
> every Wednesday at 9.30 am

We thought we would give it a go. It meant getting up a bit early which we are not good at particularly when we are on holiday but, when we arrived, it was what it said on the door. The chaplain is a lovely Welshman called Nigel Thomas.

He had set up a table amidst the ordered clutter typical of a charity shop and there he conducted Holy Communion with a small congregation taking part.

When I stepped down from lay leading our church, Sally and I went away for a month, spending most of the time there and attending communion in the Charity Shop. But then came a calamity which affected us all. Covid-19! No longer could we go to Spain so I emailed Nigel who suggested we log into a zoom meeting where he conducted Holy Communion. So for a second time we thought we would give it a try.

It took a little bit of courage to zoom into their meeting. We knew Nigel obviously and we had met the churchwarden. Other than that everybody else were complete strangers. Some lived in Spain, and others lived in the UK. From what I can gather, the "Spanish contingent" live in the hills over a wide area, whereas the "UK lot" lived anywhere from Kent to north of Aberdeen. We need not have worried, we were welcomed at the outset and soon I found myself no more amongst strangers but among friends who have helped me through the difficult times that were to follow.

I think a lot about this meeting on zoom. It is most definitely a church. It has no church building, but is a congregation of people, many of whom have never met each other in person. Yet it is a church held together by the Holy Spirit and technology unknown a few years ago. Nigel put it beautifully. It is the family of God bought together by zoom.

My church at home

Back in the UK, our church now is not the church visited by the grumpy Warden of Readers. That was a long time ago. Our current church was "Planted" from a Mother Church in

2000 and Sally and I joined them six years later. We are a church that worships in a school hall. It is a "church in a cupboard". Every Sunday morning we have to get everything out and set everything up. At the end of the service, we have to put everything away again. It is not just a question of putting the chairs out. The music and sound equipment has to be set up. Something like two hours before the service begins, two or three men with their sons, start to set up the technical equipment. I look at the faith of these lovely people working together in the work that God has given them to do. They are my joy and my crown whom I love.

Is our church a well-known church? Far from it. Do we have great preachers? Hardly. Does it get things wrong? Oh most frequently! So what is so good about it? I have come to realise that, beside God himself, there is nothing more admirable than a group of people bonded together with Jesus as their head working for the gospel. It is called the Body of Christ. People coming together with a job to do each week as they present their worship to God.

> Welcome, greeting, Bible reading
> Leading, praying with thanksgiving
> Techy, sound and audio visual
> Tea, coffee, pastoral, social
> Blessing, teaching, story telling
> Giving, counting, music, listening
> Ordination, mission and confession,
> Preparation with a thoughtful sermon.

When I see any church I go to working together, I give thanks to God and I am full of admiration. When I see my church working together, my heart misses a beat!

And God sits in the audience and applauds! We shine like the sun in his eyes!

Ananias

I want to conclude my thoughts on admiration by introducing you to an old friend. You may already know him as he may be your old friend to. His name is Ananias. I call him an old friend because he keeps popping into my mind. The reason? He shone like the sun! I have Ananias top of the list when it comes to thinking about whatever is admirable. He lived in Damascus some 2,000 years ago and is described simply as "a disciple" (Acts 9:10). Saul of Tarsus, as Paul was known then, had instructions to find anyone in Damascus who belonged to The Way, as they weren't known as Christians then (v2). So we might surmise that a church had formed there and Ananias was a member of that church. Was he a leader or just a foot soldier? We do not know and it really does not matter because what he did was quite incredible. As with others highlighted in my thoughts, Ananias is, in my view, one of the Bibles underestimated characters, which makes me think that he was more of a foot soldier. How I portray Ananias may not be to everybody's taste but it is expressed in the affectionate way that I think of him.

Ananias! Perhaps Ananias had been a soldier perhaps now retired. Certainly, he was a soldier of Christ.

Ananias! What we do know about Ananias is that, at that moment, his life was in deadly peril. Saul travelling to Damascus was probably on his hit list.

Ananias! What Ananias did not know was that the resurrected Jesus had intercepted Saul before he reached Damascus and the short exchange between them had left Saul blind.

"ANANIAS!" – Ananias was suddenly aware that this was God calling him. The warrior leapt to his feet:

"Lord! Sah!"

"Go to the house of Judas on Straight Street and ask for a man from Tarsus named Saul for he is praying. In a vision, he has seen a man named Ananias come and place his hands on him to restore his sight."

"Permission to speak, Sah!"

"Go ahead"

"My Lord, Sah! There are reports that this man has done much 'arm to your saints in Jerusalem and has come 'ere with authority to arrest all who call on your name. Sah! Beggin' your pardon, Sah!"

"Go. This man is my chosen instrument to carry my name to Gentiles, kings and the people of Israel."

"Yes Sah! Right away Sah!"

(This is an imaginative recital of the story that can be found in Acts 9:10-16.)

And that's it. He went to the house of Judas, found Saul, laid hands on him and restored his sight. Isn't that absolutely admirable? Perhaps compare this to other moments in the Bible when God has called someone specifically to do a task. Moses, the great leader of Israel, at the burning bush for instance. Was he not a trifle bothered? Or what about Zachariah, the father of John the Baptist. God rendered him dumb through his disbelief. Ananias seemed impervious. His commanding officer gave an order and Ananias obeyed. What could be simpler? A wonderful man but apparently not like me, it seems, because I am not sure that I could have done what he did.

It has struck me that Ananias must have been supremely content in his relationship with God. Ananias was where God wanted him to be. There in Damascus, a humble soldier was in the right place at the right time. He possessed, deep within his innermost soul, both a contented faith in Jesus and the humility to accept orders when they were given. If Jesus wanted him to heal his prospective murderer then that was fine with him. The command was not what Ananias wanted to hear but he was ready to obey his Lord.

Was he not just a bit worried? It is difficult to know but he certainly realised that going to Judas' house that day would probably end up in prison ready for transportation back to Jerusalem. Furthermore, Ananias would not have had the benefit, as we have, of Paul's letter to the Philippians. Yet here we have a man who stood firm. This is someone who was not anxious. A man content to do what he was told. God chose Paul, whom Ananias healed to be his "chosen instrument". Christianity therefore was handed down to all gentiles including me, because of the faith, trust and humility of Ananias. He is someone truly to be admired.

We have now reached the last "whatever" to think about in order to replace worry – thinking about whatever is excellent and praiseworthy. A painting by Rembrandt Harmenszoon van Rijn called "The Supper at Emmaus" will help me think about this "whatever". This painting will also help to form a link through to the conclusion of this book with the final challenge. "I have learned the secret of being content in any and every situation" Philippians 4:12.

Prayer. *Lord you are over all things – the great and the small. You are over the commendable actions of those who lead their everyday lives. We remember individuals and communities who have served you undertaking tasks that only your strength could fulfil. Thank you Lord for the pleasure we can get from the unassuming foot soldiers who obey, get out of their comfort zones and lead.*

Questions you might like to consider:

- Has God ever taken you out of your comfort zone? What have you learned from this?
- Do you see your worship to God being vertical or horizontal? Is God "up there" or "next door"? Do you think you are admirable in God's eyes?
- Can you see where God has enabled you to do something commendable?
- Is there someone that you have found to be admirable? In what way does this help you?
- What thoughts would you include if you wrote this chapter on whatever is admirable or commendable.

The supper at Emmaus by Rembrandt

CHAPTER TEN

THINKING ABOUT WHATEVER IS EXCELLENT AND PRAISEWORTHY

On the first day of the week very early in the morning, the women took the spices they had prepared and went to the tomb. They found the stone rolled away from the tomb but when they entered, they did not find the body of the Lord Jesus
Luke 24:–2

This has to be the most excellent and praiseworthy event ever. They could not find the body of Jesus because it was not there. God resurrected Jesus from the dead. The impact of this for us is beyond anything imaginable. It means we have life after death because of Jesus' death and resurrection. Just think for a moment what that means for each of us, if we could just put our doubts aside. It simply means that we do not have to worry about death. Nevertheless, death is the taboo subject of our generation. We do not talk about death and it always seems to take us by surprise when it comes.

"But that is so unfair, I never smoked," says a person diagnosed with lung cancer.

"I can't understand it, he was such a fitness fanatic," says the relative of someone who has died from heart disease.

We hear things said like this over and over again. The gains in medical treatment are huge and they have been able to extend our life span. More people are living over 100 years now but the plain and simple fact is that we will die – one day.

This chapter is devoted to this one event. Jesus raised from the dead.

The Louvre

We were not blessed with the best of weather, Saju and I, when we took our trip to Paris. As a result I had to head with him for the great indoors. For indoors, nothing can beat the Louvre – the largest art gallery that I have ever been to. The problem I faced is what art would my 38 year old, 6'3" cricket loving companion from South India want to see? There was so much choice. I started him on what I thought was a sure thing – the *Mona Lisa*! When we reached the room where it was displayed, Saju solemnly wedged himself in the crowd while I stood to the side and admired other paintings in the room. I looked at him, his head looming over everyone else and then, without a word, he withdrew from the crowd. I could see that the *Mona Lisa* did not do it for him! Where to go now? For a moment I was stumped, then I made the decision to take him to what I wanted to see in the hope that he would enjoy what I enjoyed – the Dutch Masters. Thankfully, I hit the bullseye. He clearly loved a small painting by Johannes Vermeer of a girl doing needlework and then he came across a Rembrandt of *Supper at the Emmaus* and this held him spellbound in what seemed hours.

The Emmaus Road

If ever there was a painting that I would want to pass by, it would be *Supper at the Emmaus*. At first, I could not see what my young friend saw in it. The Caravaggio version is much more dramatic. I stood with him for a few minutes until my back started to complain and I sat down and waited. The figures of people that feature in it are relatively small in size, only occupying the bottom half of the canvas space. The top half is dark and appears really... to be rather ugly. It is as if the painting seems to be saying – "Carry along there. The next painting is much more interesting". Is that what Rembrandt intended? Is he indicating very subtly that many pass by the most excellent and praiseworthy event in the history of the whole of humankind. I wonder – because many do.

It is a group of four figures. The central figure is Jesus seated at a table breaking bread. The other three figure are grouped around him, two of them are seated and looking at him intently. The third is looking down in a servile posture. Something very dramatic is about to happen. Rembrandt has caught the moment. You can find the full story of the Road to Emmaus in Luke 24:13–49

Jesus has been crucified. It had been a hideous death. Two disciples are walking a short seven miles from Jerusalem to a village called Emmaus. It was not really a walk but probably more of an amble as they were lost in their thoughts and their misery. The beautiful Jesus they had followed was now gone, their hopes and expectations dashed into pieces. Then unexpectedly another person joins them on the road. It was the resurrected Jesus but they did not recognise him. How could they? Jesus was dead for goodness sake! They had seen it happen with their own eyes. So, there was Jesus walking on the same road that they were walking on but they did not know who he was. They listened as the stranger explained scripture and all that had happened and they still did not grasp his identity. I am reminded of those fateful words at the beginning of John's gospel, "He (God) was in the world and, though the world was made through him, the world did not recognise him" John 1:10. This remains true to this day.

The disciples arrived at the village and, with the night drawing in, they decided, or they were destined to stop so they invited the stranger to join them. As they were about to eat together, something happened. It was when the stranger broke the bread. This is the moment depicted in the painting. It is a "still life" of an event that was anything but still. Then suddenly, they saw with absolute certainty, that the stranger was Jesus. The Man... risen from the dead! When they had recovered from the shock, Jesus was no longer there but they were completely clear in their own minds as to what they had to do. They had to return immediately to Jerusalem and tell the other disciples. We might imagine them running the seven miles back to Jerusalem arriving hot and sweaty with their news to find to their amazement that they were not alone. Peter had also seen the risen Jesus. They were excited but had no understanding of what was happening they only knew what they had witnessed with their own eyes. "The peace of God which transcends all understanding".

Jesus did not leave them with a lack of understanding long. As they talked excitedly together, they suddenly were aware that Jesus was there... among them... and now they knew exactly who he was. After they got over the initial surprise, he identified himself by showing them his hands and feet. Then any doubts was thrown aside by the question that Jesus then asked. "Has anybody got anything to eat around here. I'm hungry". How many times had they heard this before! Let us face it – I do not think he got much to eat at Emmaus.

Dinner over and they began to talk. "He opened their minds, so they could understand the scriptures" Luke 24:45. Now they understood that Jesus had risen from the dead, they began to understand the cross. Now on the other side of the resurrection, they began to see how Jesus had forged a way through death creating a path to God to all who put their faith in him and humbly accepted their need of repentance and forgiveness. There was a job to be done, a service to be offered – to preach this message to all nations. I cannot imagine they had much sleep that night! Nothing is more excellent and praiseworthy than this.

That night Jesus, resurrected in our world, fed their understanding. Now I wanted to see whether this painting could help feed my understanding. There seemed to be a strand running through this excellent and praiseworthy event. A strand made up of three parts – faith, humility and service. Like a rope entwined and unbreakable. This seems to be reflected in the letter Paul wrote to the church at Philippi. He has three strands that weave through its pages centred and held together by the creed in Philippians 2.

Our faith is in Jesus
who made himself nothing taking the
very nature of a servant.
(Faith, humility and service)

Now I began to look at Rembrandt's painting with different eyes. No longer was I looking at the painting to SEE what was in it. I was now looking at the painting to FIND something in it. I was looking at the painting to tell me something about Jesus. What might it tell me about faith, humility and service? I was also looking to see what it might say about worry.

The painting

It is the light that first grabbed my attention. It seems to come from an unidentified source from the left of the picture. An unseen window? Hardly. It was after all, meant to be night-time. The light falls on the central figure. What is about to happen is all about Jesus.

Yet there is another light. This is a light, rather like a halo, that surrounds Jesus. This light seems to separate Jesus from the others in the painting. They sit and stand in close proximity but they are somehow apart from him. I notice the sorrow on Jesus' face. It is as if he yearns for them to recognise who he is and what he has done. What they saw at Calvary was not just a man dying on a cross of crucifixion. What they saw, without knowing, was the Son of God taking their sins, your sins and mine on the cross and dying. Now he is raised from the dead and seated in their presence, and yet still they do not know who he is. No wonder Jesus is looking sorrowful. However, the next moment all that changed. In a moment, they would know without any doubt that he was alive.

I followed the light down the painting and I see that, as well as falling on Jesus, it also falls as predominantly on the table. Although it is low and relatively humble for a table, yet it holds a prominence in the painting with the light shining on it. The design of the table allows for people to get their legs under it and get close. The table is laid and, though humble, has what seems to be a rather sumptuous cover laid over its surface and this is partially protected by a white tablecloth. It all seems to indicate that something special was about to happen here. The table is sparse, plates and knives are laid before the three people seated. There is no candelabra or table decorations. No fine drinking goblets. I get the impression from the sparseness that no one anticipated being there for long. This place of meeting was going to lead to somewhere else. Somewhere better.

The table depicts the place where they met and talked with Jesus. The table is represented today by the altar in our churches, although the altars we have today are usually much grander than this humble table depicted at Emmaus. At the altar, we gather and meet with Jesus where bread is broken at Holy Communion. Many Christians were denied Communion during covid lockdown but we must never forget that the table exists in our hearts where Jesus can meet with us at any time.

Now, lost in my own thoughts, I began to ponder what the three people around the table might represent. The man seated to the right of Jesus might represent Faith. The person to the left of Jesus might represent Humility and the person who is standing might represent Service. In my mind, I see Jesus inviting them to join him at the table where he can give them redemption, their separation from God. These three people have a common purpose. They are concentrating their whole being on Jesus. They are not in any way concerned about where they are.

The background behind and below the group is dark and stark and not at all welcoming. Not the sort of place you would invite Jesus to stay with you. Even the floorboards look like they would give splinters to any bare feet that dared to venture across them. It is also out of proportion. Jesus looks like he is sitting under some sort of giant vault and then, if you look at the door, it is far too tall if you compare it to the height of the standing man. It looks like they are breaking bread in a dungeon for giants! I thought of Psalm 23: "You prepare a table before me in the presence of my enemies" Psalm 23:5.

What has come out of this painting for me is that Jesus is sharing his communion in the presence of our enemies. We bring our Faith, our Humility, our Service to him at the table in the presence of giants – and worry is foremost. Yet not just worry – all giants are represented in this stark unwelcoming room. Fear and guilt. Pride and jealousy. Anger and lack of confidence. Frustration and confusion. Jesus comes to us where we are knowing our struggles with these giants. The people in the painting are not looking at what is around them. They are looking at Jesus. We celebrate communion with Jesus in the presence of worry, yet Jesus is bigger than worry.

I will praise you O lord with all my heart
before the "gods" I will sing your praise
I will bow down toward your holy temple
and will praise your name
for your love and your faithfulness
for you are exalted above all things
your name and your word.
When I called, you answered me
you made me bold and stout hearted.
Psalm 138:1-3

This is my prayer as we think about whatever is excellent and praiseworthy.

Going forward

Thinking about these "whatever's" should never finish while we have life on this Earth. It should be a continual process because replacing worry is a constant requirement. However, there is another "whatever" that follows this list of God-characteristics. It takes us to the end of this study and to Paul's final claim about finding contentment. Paul writes, "Whatever you have learned or received or heard from me, or seen in me – put it into practice" Philippians 4:9. So, we must exercise replacing worry with this list of God-characteristics every day – and more than that. We must put into practice all that Paul has written in his letter.

I continue to look at Rembrandt's painting *Supper at Emmaus* and I am asking myself a big question. If I complete this exercise thinking about whatever is true, whatever is noble, whatever is just, pure, lovely admirable – excellent and praiseworthy, will I be content? I am confident that the exercise would bring a big, big stride in the right direction because we cannot be content while we are worrying. So transcending worry, at the very least, lays a foundation stone toward contentment. However, I am

concerned that thinking about whatever is true, noble etc...
equals... contentment. This sounds altogether too formulaic.
Paul describes contentment in Philippians 4:12 as being a secret.
I am drawn to the thought that contentment depends on other
factors being involved.

Questions you might like to consider:

- What is the recipe for excellence in your world?
- What is the significance of praising God?
- Is there someone that you know who is praiseworthy?
  Can you emulate that?
- Does praising the excellence of God give you peace?
- What thoughts would you include if you wrote this
  chapter on whatever is excellent and praiseworthy?

CHAPTER ELEVEN
FAITH

*Now faith is being sure of what we hope
for and certain of what we do not see*
Hebrews 11:1

Three people gathered around Jesus. The two seated had walked from Jerusalem to a village called Emmaus. In Luke chapter 24 they are described as "downcast" and well they might be. All their hopes and dreams were dashed. Their faith in Jesus of Nazareth lay in tatters, killed off cruelly by a Roman cross of death. On the way, they had met a stranger who walked with them and explained from the scriptures why these things happened. They listened and their heart burned within them but they did not understand. In their bewilderment, they did not recognise the stranger as Jesus who was in the process of breaking bread.

Faith – Rembrandt's man seated to the right.

I want this chapter to concentrate on the man seated to the right of Jesus as we look at it. We might imagine that this man represents Faith – our faith. The first thing that we might notice is that the light does not fall directly on this man as it does on Jesus or the table. We might describe him as being in the shadow, neither light nor dark, the side of his body away from Jesus is disappearing into the darkness of the background. It might be seen to represent the wreckage of his faith. He is in a dark place with no light in the tunnel. His hope in Jesus was crushed. He is in the "Valley of the Shadow of Death" (see Psalm 23:4) and perhaps he lives in fear of what is around the corner. His dreams had seemingly come to nothing. He cannot see where to go next. Nothing comforts him. He stares at the stranger breaking bread and questions in his mind.

He is sitting upright – bolt upright. His body looks tense not leaning toward Jesus or away. He is in a "don't know" position. But his right hand is on the table holding a napkin. This may represent all he is able to bring – his wrecked faith. Sometimes that is all we can do. Jesus wants us to bring our faith to the table however small, weak or wrecked it might be.

I relate to this man. I can come to Jesus' table and bring the wreckage of my faith. Yet that is OK. That is enough. The risen Jesus is at the table, ready to receive us no matter how let down we have been or how much our lives have been devastated. Jesus is there even if we have turned away from him or committed, in our eyes, terrible acts of sin. In Matthew's gospel, we find that famous verse "If you have faith as small as a mustard seed you can say to this mountain 'Move from there' – and it will move" Matthew17:20. A mustard seed is very, very small. It only takes a very, very small amount of faith to move God, and God in Jesus is a very big mountain.

That moment they recognised Jesus. We might imagine gasps, the sound of chairs being pushed back as they stood gaping in amazement, plate and food crash to the floor. And then... he's gone! That moment was enough. They had seen Jesus for sure and they recalled together what had taken place on the road. Their faith had found new life. It holds a message for all struggling in life.

The Valley of Rocks

I find it impossible to define how faith begins in a person. Where do we begin to be "certain of things unseen"? Hebrews 11:1 Where did we first know that Jesus was God in the world and that he died to save us from our sins and then to rise again so we can rise with him? When did the penny drop? It seems that everyone has a different apology for their faith. When I became a Christian, it seemed that we were expected to relate to a moment when we asked Jesus into our life. Testimonies were trotted out and it all left me rather cold. For me, there was no "moment". I became a Christian through listening, contemplating and wrestling over what I did not understand. I realised, at a very early stage, that we become Christians in different ways. I thought that the well-known Christmas stories had something to tell us about this. I thought of different ways people found the baby Jesus. The shepherds had an exhilarating experience. They would be like those who have experienced a moment of revelation. On the other hand, we have the Magi who saw a star rise in the east and went in search to find out what it meant. This was a long journey and took time. That would be more like my journey to faith. Then there is Mary and Joseph who found Jesus through a great deal of pain and suffering. Finally old Simeon who found Jesus after years of waiting. However, God did not leave me without a revelation moment in my early Christian years. Perhaps he thought I needed one in order to help keep my faith on track in difficult times. Others, less doubting than me, might not need such an experience. As I have said, we are all different.

A lot of my early Christian learning came from house parties that were run each year by my first church. This would involve a large group of young people staying in a lovely house originally built for someone wealthy who wanted a country pad but was now used as a private primary school. The day came when a coach had been booked for a trip to the Valley of the Rocks. This is a beautiful, rugged spot with high cliffs overlooking the sea in North Devon. Michael (not his real name) was on that house party. He was slightly older than I was and suffered from epilepsy. I remember Michael when first introduced to him in church. He had a novel method of solving problems.

"You have your say, John and then I will have my say and then we shall see what the Bible says," explained Michael. I did not think that was quite fair as, at the time, I hadn't a clue what the Bible said about anything!

On the day of the outing, a coach dropped the house party within walking distance from the cliff edge. I nervously looked over the edge. It was a long way down – a sheer vertical drop to a rocky shore and the sea. Overcoming my fear of heights,

I turned to go back to the coach when the most terrible news reached us. Michael had suffered an epileptic fit and had fallen off the edge of the cliff. Everyone got back into the coach and feverishly prayed to God. A crowd had gathered on the cliff top watching the helicopter from RNAS Culdrose hovering overhead while the house party was praying. I confess that my thoughts were not positive.

"What's the point? Michael is dead. No one could survive a fall from that height".

Then, after what seemed ages, one of the house party leaders got on the coach. "Michael is alive!" he said. That's impossible!

"He fell onto a ledge part way down," explained the leader. Michael indeed was alive and went on to recover, get married, and father a baby girl.

Some years later, I returned to the Valley of the Rocks only this time I walked around the bottom of the cliff. Looking up, I could see the ledge that Michael had fallen onto, that I could not see from the top. It was still quite a tumble but amazingly Michael had dropped and stayed on the ledge rather than rolling off and onto the shore below. I could only wonder in living hope at the miracle that had happened that day at the Valley of the Rocks.

I learned a great deal about faith that day. I learned that my faith did not rely on that experience; my faith is imbedded within me by the Holy Spirit. This experience is one of several that I can look on and remember. The other lesson was that I could not see the ledge. This did not mean that it was not there. This is, for me, an illustration of faith. Being certain in what we cannot see. I may not be able to see God in what I am going through but he is there. In later life, I was to go through another valley – the valley of the shadow of death. My journey that tested my faith had begun.

Faith challenged – beginning John's final story

Twenty-one years ago, I was diagnosed with prostate cancer. The news completely rocked me. I had never had a moment of illness in my life let alone a life-threatening one. Like the parable of the rich man who suddenly died (see chapter eleven) – it was terribly inconvenient! It was felt that the cancer should be treated with radiotherapy and drugs. By and large, nothing really happened after that. I went to see a very nice London Hospital based professor every three or six months and all was well

In March 2020 when the first lockdown came into force, God had nudged me to write this book about the Philippian passage following Matt's talk. I was able to start writing knowing that I had Saju's help. I presented Saju with the first draft and we both realised that this was just a beginning. There was much more to be done. That night I stood up to go to bed and suddenly felt the room spinning round like a "carousel".

"Get down to A & E straight away" advised a 24-hour doctor service.

"Surely not. Perhaps tomorrow morning," I remonstrated.

"Now!" came back the emphatic reply.

It was a worrying ordeal to be undertaken alone as Covid rules forbade Sally coming into hospital with me. Five hours later Sally collected me from A & E. The duty registrar had put me through test after test, and eventually informed me that I had suffered a stroke. It affected my sight and balance. My sight problem meant that I would never drive again and the balance problems manifested themselves later so that I had to walk with a stick and rely on a mobility scooter.

That expression "It never rains but it pours" began to come to my mind. Shortly after my return from hospital came a knock at the door. It was my neighbour from the apartment downstairs.

"John," he said, "There's water coming into our apartment".

Sally went to look and, sure enough, water was coming through their ceiling and down the walls. Our bathroom appliances had been all built-in so that it was impossible to detect a fault without removing some of the bathroom tiling. An emergency plumber plugged the leak and revealed to us that the appliances in both bathrooms needed to be replaced. After some consideration, we awarded the contract to replace the appliances to a firm of bathroom specialists.

Work began on our bathrooms at the beginning of December. The job was going to take two weeks to complete.

"It will all be done by Christmas," we thought.

The contractors came for the first week during which they removed all the appliances leaving us with running water and one working toilet before going off for the weekend. At 7.30am on Monday morning of the second week, the phone rang and Sally answered.

"Mrs Bloor," said the voice of the contractor at the other end of the phone, "I'm sorry but we won't be able to come this morning in fact we won't be able to finish the job until mid-January. We've all gone down with Covid!" We now looked forward to an unwashed Christmas! A few days later, we both began to show symptoms of the virus. This, of course, was before any vaccinations were available and death rates in this country were at around 2,000 per day. Through all this, I was trying to complete the second draft of the book. "Don't be anxious about anything," wrote Paul to the Philippian church. Are you sure? My faith was being challenged.

There then came a defining moment. I hobbled out onto my balcony and prayed. My prayer was short and stark. Looking up at the night sky, I said, "Lord, if you want me to finish this book, don't let us cough". It was a heartfelt prayer as infections of any kind seemed always to go to my chest and I knew that might risk a serious covid infection. But God granted my request. WE DID NOT COUGH. We shivered and shook, then sweated and shivered again. On Christmas Day the fever broke. We ate our Christmas dinner alone, as many did that year, and Sally could not taste a thing!

The New Year 2021 saw the contactors back, now fully recovered and ready to finish off the bathrooms. Of more concern was my continued inability to walk. An MRI scan showed an arthritic back and this was thought to be the main problem,

"You've got to exercise more," said the consultant encouragingly, as I hobbled out of his consulting room. A chiropractor was unconvinced and suggested a hip X-ray. The result revealed that the cartilage in my right hip had completely worn away. It was little wonder that I was in so much pain. In July, after a start/stop experience with the NHS, I had a full hip replacement operation. Rendered completely numb from the waist down but otherwise conscious throughout, a wonderful surgeon and his team gave me a new hip while the anaesthetist told me some really awful jokes to keep me entertained. It was a surreal experience.

Regrettably, there were complications. I became breathless and my feet, ankles and legs swelled up. My doctor diagnosed heart failure. I was plagued with nerve pain and there were other problems. I will not go into detail other than it would leave women nodding in understanding and men wincing! I wondered what might come next.

Like the man in the Rembrandt painting, my days seemed to be long and dark, with no end in sight. I was puzzled, as I seemed to be hit by one thing after another. "Where are you God?" was a question not far from my lips. Contentment was not part of my daily life. Yet worse was to come – much worse. My faith felt like it was being tested to the limit.

CHAPTER TWELVE
HUMILITY

Humble yourselves under God's might hand
so that he will lift you up in his own good time.
Leave your worries with him because he cares for you
1 Peter 5:6–7

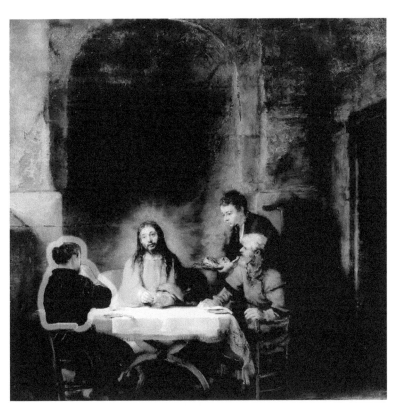

I am now looking at the figure seated to the left of Jesus as we look at the painting of Rembrandt's *Supper at Emmaus*. This is a difficult figure to make out because the body dressed in dark clothes is half turned away from us, sitting forward on the edge of the chair and totally absorbed in Jesus. To my untutored eye, this could be the figure of a woman. It matters not, as what this person might represent applies to all people from all nations, male and female.

The light comes in from the left falling mainly on Jesus and the table and missing the person seated to the left of Jesus who therefore is in darkness all except one feature... the hands! The light shows that the hands are together as if in prayer with the right elbow resting on the table. This person, to me, represents humility. Before the Lord, hands together beseeching, entreating. Lord help me... Lord save me... Lord guide me... Lord have mercy. On the right, faith is present through the man's hand resting on the table but leaning back. On the contrary, this person representing humility is leaning forward even perhaps ready to reach out and touch Jesus. In their different ways, in their different postures, both are directed toward the central figure breaking bread, "This is my body given for you" (Luke 22:19).

Humility is so misunderstood. Unforgiving stubbornness is truly terrible. It leaves hatred and misery in its wake. Far from being strong, it often leads to lives that are broken and leading nowhere. Humility on the other hand looks like weakness. It rides blows and insults but in fact opens doors that which may have been stubbornly shut. Humility brings people together at war with each other and achieves healing where sickness prevails. In the creed set out in Philippians 2:7, it is said of Jesus, "He made himself nothing, taking the very nature of a servant". There is a very gritty Bible story in Matthew 15:21–28 and tells of a woman whose faith and humility gave her the desire of her heart.

Humility is in perseverance

She came from Tyre and Sidon, which is north of Galilee in the region of Phoenicia. She is known in Matthew's gospel as the "Canaanite woman" whereas Mark, singles her out as Greek. One way or the other, she was not of Jewish stock and this is an important feature in this story. Her young daughter had mental issues described by the mother as demon-possession. Word about Jesus had got out. If anybody could heal her daughter from her dreadful affliction, Jesus could. She then learned that Jesus had travelled from Galilee and was in the vicinity. If only she could get to him but the question was – would he see her? She was desperate.

Jesus, on the other hand, wanted a break. He had been at Gennesaret on the Sea of Galilee and people flocked to him bringing their sick. Their demands and a typical tangle with the Pharisees had left him needing to withdraw. The coastal area around Tyre and Sidon seemed perfect. This might explain the hostile atmosphere the Canaanite woman met when she found where Jesus was staying.

I have an image that it was after dark and a fire had been lit. Supper had been served and Jesus and the disciples were sitting eating on the ground. Dogs were a familiar sight padding around the outskirts of the camp darting in when they could grab a morsel or two left over by the diners. That is where she was – with the dogs, coming in when she saw an opportunity, begging and yet, being driven off. She was persistent in what she was doing and eventually the disciples got fed up with her. "For goodness sake send her away," they moaned to Jesus. Jesus seemed to agree. "I was only sent to the lost sheep of Israel," which seems to identify her cause as undeserving. In spite of this, she gets to speak to Jesus.

Lord help me.
It's not right to take the children's bread
and toss it to the dogs
Yes Lord but even the dogs eat the crumbs
that fall from their masters table
(Taken from Matthew 15:25–27)

What an answer! An unexpected response from a gentile. It is difficult to know, but I imagine even Jesus was taken aback. After all, he was wholly human as well as being wholly God. "Woman, you have great faith! Your request is granted," (v28) and, we are told that the daughter, who was not even there, was healed immediately.

"We are not worthy to gather up the crumbs under your table," is what we say in the prayer of Humble Access before we take Communion. Jesus commended her faith but her powerhouse was in her humility. Her faith kept her in the camp and from there she was able to reach out to Jesus in humility.

Humility is in waiting

Saju recognised the importance of humility. When he first arrived as our vicar, he called together an all-day meeting of every leader in both churches. He wanted us to think about humility that day. I was at first a bit disappointed. Surely, we might think about a glorious way forward but Saju knew of his total dependence on God and asked us that day to wait on and continue to wait on the Lord. Sometime after Saju told me this story.

In 2014 Saju was walking in hills of Cumbria but he wasn't just taking the air or admiring the scenery. Actually, he wasn't much aware of anything around him because he was wrestling with a problem. It was some five or six years now since he had become ordained and he had served his curacy in Lancaster. Now he was ready for the next step. The problem was – what was the next step? Where are my gifts?

He prayed, "Lord, what sort of priest do you want me to be?".

Saju was asking this very important question. It was a humble question. He was opening himself to find out the truth of his future ministry. It could have differed from the truth he might have preferred.

He had woken up at home with Katy and turned, as he did every morning, to his daily Bible reading. It was from Psalm 27:14, "Wait for the Lord, be strong and take heart," and, with the verse on his mind, set off on his walk. When he reached Borrowdale, he sat down and began to listen and ponder a sermon by Stuart McAllister. His text was; "Wait for the Lord, be strong and take heart".

Saju sensed that the apparent coincidence heralded that the Lord was near and knew all about his problem. Suitably encouraged he started back for home. On his way back, he got a text from Katy. She heard that morning from a friend who felt that she had something to tell Saju. It was important; something that God had laid on her heart. This friend was not normally given to expressing herself this way, but God was urging her. "Saju, look at Psalm 27 – Wait for the Lord, be strong and take heart!" Saju waited and the Lord led him first to us and then from us to Loughborough.

Humility is receiving

Like all of God's gifts to us, humility is multi-faceted. Humility is forbearing and persevering, humility is waiting. Humility also knows how to receive. Sometimes receiving is not easy.

For instance, I recall, not long before I retired, the first time when someone stood up in the London underground to offer me their seat. I recall another time.

My health problems had combined to make walking a continued difficulty. I could walk all right. It was just that I could only walk slowly. It was on one of my little walks which I do every Sunday to church when I was accosted by two little boys who I didn't know. "'ere, mister, do you want one of these?" and one of the boys held out a Tupperware box within which were a number of chocolate brownies.

"Well thank you," I replied, "I won't eat it now but I will when I get to church" and I went on my way. It was a curious thing to happen but I thought nothing of it until the homeward journey.

The church service over and I started my slow walk back home. A young girl came the other way as I neared my front door. There was a lot of shouting going on nearby with some dragon boat racing. I said to the girl as she passed, "Have you been to see the racing?"

She replied, "No but I'm going this afternoon," and then asked, "Would you like an apple?" and with that her hand dived into her coat pocket and drew out a Golden Delicious apple.

"Thank you," I said, "I'll eat it with my lunch".

Now I was curious. Why had the children who I did not know, offer me their sweets and their fruit? Perhaps they saw a great need in me but I did not think I looked too decrepit! I cannot answer that question but I felt that the important thing was my reaction. I could have said, "No thank you very much," and passed up their help. Instead, I humbly received and rejoiced about it afterwards as I told friends and family.

Humility is accepting

I think this is one of the more difficult facets about humility. Having to humbly accept what you might not want to accept.

Andrew is with God now and he was my friend. He was churchwarden at the Parish Church but he, his wife and two children started coming to our church as well. The family were quite at home in both the formality of the Parish Church and the informality of our church. He joined my home group and we all quickly grasped his intelligence. When we were stuck, we would always ask Andrew for guidance. In the meantime, his children joined in with the mid-week teenage group. Saju, Andrew and I were all school governors. It was not a post that I particularly relished but Andrew was always on hand to help me through – particularly with the techy stuff!

Then one day he drew me aside and told me that he had been diagnosed with terminal cancer. "My life can be prolonged with chemo," he said. He lived for a further three years and became more and more involved with Saju and my church in that time. He was completely reliable.

"Andrew can you go into Sunday school this morning? Someone hasn't turned up".

He never complained about his condition, but only to express sorrow that he would not see his children grow up. Andrew lived close by so I was a frequent visitor. We would talk about his treatment but we would also talk about church problems and gradually, without any forward planning, he became my mentor. God had provided someone to help me through some very difficult issues that arose during my leadership.

Remarkably, he never looked unwell. In his last month, he turned up at Messy Church as he always did – ready to help, he looked fine but tired. He died just days before I stood down as leader. He was there for me right to the end.

What I love about all these reflections on humility is that worry is nowhere near any of them. Even the gritty story of the Canaanite woman because, through her humility, she was focused totally on what she had to do for her daughter. For me, that says a lot about humility. Andrew humbly accepted where his life was leading and spent the time serving the Lord, which leads me to go further with my story. As I tell it, I have Andrew constantly in mind.

Continuing John's story

In humility, I had to accept what was happening to me. In humility, I had to accept what was going to happen to me. I did not realise how hard this was going to be. I had suffered a stroke, I couldn't walk properly and needed a hip replacement. The problem exposed other problems, which in turn created problems with my kidneys. My heart was struggling to move fluid around my body and I suffered excruciating nerve pain in my right leg. What else could go wrong? I did not have long to find out.

It was the doctor, treating me for the nerve pain, who first rang the alarm.

"John, I want you to go for a bone scan."

"Why do I need a bone scan?"

"It is the prostate cancer."

"Oh, no problems there. It has been asleep for 21 years."

"I think we had better do a scan."

The cancer was out. It had decided to join the party. The bone scan revealed that it had spread extensively into my spine. The blood test showed that it was aggressive. A few months later while on holiday with Sally, I received notification of my youngest son's unexpected and untimely death. He had decided to end his life. He was 48 years old and about to start a new job.

We are hard pressed on every side, but not crushed. Perplexed, but not in despair; persecuted, but not abandoned; struck down but not destroyed 2 Corinthians 4:8–9

CHAPTER THIRTEEN
SERVICE

*About the third hour he went out and saw
others standing in the market place doing nothing.
He told them 'You go and work in my vineyard'*

I am curious about the man standing in Rembrandt's *Supper at Emmaus*. Most of his body is obscured because he is standing behind the man seated to the right of Jesus – he who represents faith, to my eyes, albeit a faith that has gone through the mangle. The standing man is serving and seems not to want to be noticed and indeed, while I was positioned beside Saju looking at the painting in the Louvre, Paris, I really didn't take much notice of him either. He is obsequiously bowed, his eyes turned downward and a tray is in his hand with supper on it. He does not touch the table because he is serving at the table but his face is lit up! I find that strange because the is light coming from the left and goes nowhere near his face. Yet, with the exception of Jesus, it is his face that is more alight than those he is serving. The light on his face might be coming from the light that surrounds Jesus. Here Rembrandt has painted a servant or the mythological Emmaus innkeeper yet the account in Luke's gospel gives no indication where they were staying. This image might show that when we serve, we might serve unnoticed. It shows us that serving Jesus can light us up. I am drawn to the image that the man representing Service stands behind the seated man representing Faith. The enigma of service is divulged perhaps through a rather obscure parable that Jesus told in Matthew 20:1-1.

The workers in the vineyard

This little-known parable holds, in my view, a very important lesson in our understanding of Service. It is little known, because it is difficult to understand. It starts with those familiar words that so often begin parables "The Kingdom of Heaven is like..." (v1) and finishes with many very disgruntled people! (see v11) So let me re-tell it.

There was a landowner and he owned a vineyard. He woke up early one morning with the sun shining and the grapes were ripe so he went early and hired some workers to harvest the grapes. He agreed to pay them a denarius for the day. I do not think it matters how much a denarius is worth in today's money. The main point is that the workers were happy with their wages. Three hours later, he realised his need of more workers. Now the narrative is very important at this point if we are to understand the parable. The Bible says, "He went out and saw others in the market place doing nothing" (v4). The Bible says that he would pay them what was right. They must have trusted the landowner because they agreed to those terms. Three hours later, and the landowner needed even more workers and "he went out again" (v5) and then the same again three hours after that. It was now coming late in the day and the landowner realised that still more workers were required. He went out yet again at the eleventh hour.

"Hey you!"

"You mean me?"

"Yes. Have you been just standing around here all day?"

"Nobody has hired us yet."

"Well get into my vineyard now" (taken from v 6–7),

It was now late, there was only one hour left in the day to harvest the grapes (v12.) Evening came and it was wages-time when something rather unexpected happened. The landowner summons his foreman to him – his instructions were explicit. All the workers were to be paid just the same amount – one denarius (v10)

That did not go down well with those hired toward the beginning of the day. They began to grumble. A spokesperson spoke up, "Why should those (meaning the workers hired later in the day) get paid the same as us? They have only worked a few hours at the end of the day when the sun was going down whereas we have worked through the day while the sun was hot" (v12).

However, the landowner was unmoved. "They agreed a denarius so be happy with a denarius". He could do what he wanted with his money, couldn't he? (v15) Then, to cap it all, payment was to be conducted in reverse order. Those hired last were to be paid first, and those hired first who had been working all day and were probably anxious to bathe, were to stand and wait. They would be last in the queue (v8).

Unfair or what!!? Is this the kingdom of heaven? The landowner clearly represents God and the workers represent those who work in some way or other for his kingdom here on earth. I have heard explanations along the line that this is a parable about God's grace – that he is gracious and generous to those who have worked lesser hours. Well that may be the case but, for me, it does not stack up.

For years, I never understood this parable. Then one morning in church, one of the leaders was trying to explain the parable. In spite of the fact that I did not hear the explanation, the penny dropped. I had "a frustrated eureka moment". Instead of running down the street naked and shouting "Eureka – I have found it," as Aristotle did, I had to button my lip. I wanted to stand up, move to the lectern, and ask the preacher to move over while I took over. My arrogant moment was over so I told Sally instead.

The landowner represents God and we are the workers. The important thing to understand is where everybody was. God was in the vineyard coming into "the marketplace" where the workers were. He took some of the workers but left others still there. He returned and took more and so on. The workers were either in the vineyard working or in the marketplace waiting. They were not home, mowing the lawn or having a quiet moment watching the telly. If the workers had not been in the market place, then they would not have been available when the landowner returned. Only if they remained in the marketplace, could they be hired to work in the vineyard. What this parable demonstrates is far from unfair, rather it demonstrates God's justice. All the workers in the parable, worked the same hours available to them, either in the vineyard or waiting in the market place.

Yet this parable holds an even greater message than a demonstration of God's justice. It shows that in serving the Lord we all have a purpose. Some find that purpose quickly. Others have to wait, and that wait can be long and frustrating as we seek out what God wants us to do. Look at Saju's story in chapter 12 as he sought the Lord waiting to be, "ordered into the vineyard". I have served the Lord for many years. Now I have retired, does my life have any further purpose? The question is totally irrelevant. All that matters is that I am ready and waiting in the market place.

The final lesson to be learned from this excellent parable is why the first were last and those hired last were paid first. Perhaps we might answer this question to ourselves. Who had the hardest day? Those who laboured all day in the vineyard or those who waited for at least part of the day, waiting, wondering, hoping, humbly accepting that whereas there is no work now, their moment would come.

"Humble yourselves under God's mighty hand so that he will lift you up in his own good time" (1 Peter 5:6). I think this is a hard thing to do. Wait. I would suggest that waiting for hours to find the purpose of their service – might be the hardest day. In this event, perhaps a reason why they got paid first.

There are many lessons to be learned from this parable about service, but one thought comes to mind. Just supposing that the two people who walked with Jesus on the Emmaus Road all stayed at this Inn. Here is the Innkeeper holding a platter of food, serving them. This was then going to be a real moment in time for the innkeeper to serve God. For God came into the room and sat at table and broke bread. An extraordinary moment, perhaps he would fix a blue plaque on the wall of his Inn saying, "God stayed here". It just happened to be one of those moments we all know of, being in the right place at the right time, crucially ready to serve our God. We might say that the Innkeeper was in the market place, waiting, ready to serve. It is a salutatory thought that we must be ready at all times to serve and perhaps in unexpected places.

John's story concluded

Richard's mother and I (from my first marriage) have, for the past 30 years, known about the possibility that Richard would one day take his own life. At a relatively young age he had been diagnosed bi-polar. In spite of this, the condition was stabilised with drugs. Rich was also a very intelligent man rising in the field of conservation in a job that consumed his considerable energy and gave him deep satisfaction so that, when it happened, it took us by surprise. I recall that my reaction to this terrible news was muted. I suppose I really did not know what to do with it but I was now carrying a heavy load. Not only was I facing a serious medical condition, but I was also dealing with huge emotional distress. It was more that I could carry.

The telephone rang. It was my consultant oncologist. She told me of some concerns that a scan had thrown up in my spine. I was to get to A&E immediately where they were to start a series of five sessions of radiotherapy. It is difficult to understand quite what happened next but while in A&E,

I think my body said to itself, "Oh this is a hospital. I think I will park myself here for a while". Anyway, hospital is where I stayed for the next five weeks.

That first week was strange. I remember quite lot about it but not necessarily in the right order. I remember being in a lot of pain and making a lot of noise. I recall that I cried a lot and hoped that I was not disturbing too many people. Sally told me that I slept a lot. I remember being sick and them having something pushed up my nose and into my stomach to overcome this. All very unpleasant. I also remember reading the complete *Oberammergau* script and I am not sure how I managed that. (Oberammergau, a small alpine village, which hosts a passion play every ten years to give thanks for their delivery from the plague in mediaeval times. I hoped to go to Oberammergau but covid got in the way).

The following week. I had quite a few hospital staff coming to my bed. "Are you OK now, John? We got worried about you." Some came with "Do you remember me? We met last week." I did not always remember who they were. I had no idea that I had caused that much concern.

If the first week was strange, then the weeks following in hospital might be seen as even stranger. The care shown to me by the nursing and support staff was exemplary. However, those dealing with my medical conditions were probably spot-on when dealing with data analysis and diagnosis, but I began to see signs of deep unawareness over handling of my personal feelings and humanity. This became painfully aware when I was not called for the fifth radiotherapy session. The reason was never explained to me, but I was aware that the long holiday weekend for the Queen's funeral came at the same time. Again, when I raised it the following week, I was told I had four sessions and that was probably enough. I could have the fifth one if I wanted it but it was probably too late to have any effect as time had elapsed since the fourth session. What did I want to do? How did I know what to do? I had the fifth one anyway. This was not all. The hospital wanted to carry out a minor procedure on my bladder. It was all booked but cancelled without explanation. Re-booked and cancelled again. Four times it was cancelled. Then it became clear that it was not actually needed immediately anyway. It was all rather unsettling.

Then came the big one. Arrangements had been made for me to receive a phone call, following up on the cancer. It was a routine call arranged before I went into hospital and it was envisaged that I would be at home with Sally present. In the event, I was alone in an open but Covid ward. The voice at the end of the phone introduced the subject by giving me a series of numbers relating to various bits of me that were all going southwards and concluded that I had only weeks to live.

"I am very, very sorry Mr Bloor but there is nothing more that we are able to do. Goodbye."

I felt like someone who had just failed a job application.

I suppose this feeling was similar to the news of Richard's suicide. I was not aware of any particular reaction. The anger that I would experience came later. In the hospital bed, I sat muted before I picked up the telephone to break the news to Sally. Later that evening, a nurse announced to the ward that we all had to do a covid test. We all tested positive. We were going to be moved to a covid ward. However, the decision made was to leave us in our small wing, we became the covid ward. From now on, no more visitors, the doors were kept shut.

That night, I woke at around 2am. I was uncomfortable. My spinal cancer condition meant that I found it difficult to move.

I looked for my buzzer to ask for help from the nursing staff on duty but was unable to locate it. Regrettably, it had slipped behind my shoulders and I could not see it or reach it. I called to the other patients on the ward asking if they could use their buzzer to reach the nursing staff but no one replied. I cannot blame them. The ward that I was on was a medical ward reserved for the elderly. I confess that at this point, I lost it. I freaked out. I screamed and yelled and cried – all at a shut door. When I came to a modicum of sense, I managed to find my phone and called Sally who in turn rang the hospital switchboard who, after a while, were able to reach the ward. The nursing staff arrived to find a gibbering heap, crying and in utter despair.

I had reached the bottom of the pit that I had been falling into for the past two years since suffering a stroke. I could fall no further. It was there at my all-time lowest, that I began to understand what Paul might have meant when he wrote, "I have learnt to be content in all circumstances.

CHAPTER FOURTEEN
THE COSMOS OF SOULS

I shall dwell in the house of the Lord forever Psalm 23:6

I have a question to answer in this chapter. Is it possible to say that I have found contentment in all circumstances? Can I put my hand up and conclude in this book that I have found the secret of contentment in any and every situation? Right now, I am at the bottom of the pit I have been falling into for the past two years.

I was in a wretched place. King David calls it "The Valley of the Shadow of Death", (Psalm 25:4) I couldn't put it better. I seemed surrounded by mountains that I could not move. Darkness I could not illuminate. My thoughts turned to Jesus when he was facing the cross. How he must have felt. It was as if God had allowed me to experience a smidgeon of what Jesus went through. At first, I wondered if that thought was a trifle arrogant until I recalled in 1 Peter 4:13 when Peter wrote "But rejoice inasmuch that you participate in the suffering of Christ so that you may be overjoyed when his glory is revealed.

I felt faced with some sort of choice. I could either stay wallowing at the bottom or get myself out. The problem was I did not know how to do that. Trying to extricate myself from the Valley of the Shadow of Death was beyond my ability. I needed help from someone who could get into that dark valley with me, someone who had been through it before and knew where I was. Someone bigger, stronger and more powerful than me. I needed Jesus and what he gave me was not what I expected.

(Substituted names have been used in this section of the chapter)

It started with some male bonding man-talk! The point is that Connor was in the ward with me the night that I was very distressed and hit the bottom. He knew I was a Christian and saw me reduced to a gibbering heap, but from his own health problems, he reached out to me. It was the beginning.

I remembered another man called Terry a patient in the bed next to me. Terry was someone that I did not really take to at first. He was on the phone constantly seemingly sorting out his multi-million business. When he had finished he whipped back the curtains that divided our beds and told me that he would like to tell me all about his problems.

I firmly declined. "Terry I am not interested in your health problems any more than you would be interested in mine," I closed Terry down. Later in the day, I noted how Terry was dealing with his impending discharge. I was so impressed with his patience and told him so.

"Terry." I said, "I am going to pray for you – dear God I pray for Terry, please help him get his discharged quickly".

I have no idea what Terry thought nor anyone else. Later on Terry helped me get classical music on some app called Spotify (what will they think of next!)

Therefore, you might imagine how I felt when few days later I got a letter. Opening it, I found that it was a card from Terry. I was amazed. It took me a while to think of who he was but he remembered me and took the trouble to send me a get-well card. I was so surprised. I realised we can never know what impression we might make on someone.

I recalled Wendy, an administrator in the hospital coming to speak to me as I lay on a bed outside radiotherapy. I did not know Wendy but she took the time to speak to me for about 20 minutes while I described my experiences in the hospital that day. Physio had turned up to help me get up out of bed. It unfortunately coincided with a visit from Palliative Care, intent on talking to me about the options open to me when I left the hospital. Next to me was a patient his voice was demandingly strident. The interview, such as it was, went something like this:

"John you have the option of going home."

"Nurse, have you found my walking stick?"

"It sounds like the best option…"

"And it's got writing on it…"

"Or perhaps consider a nursing home"

"And what about my slippers, I can't find them…"

Needless to say, no decision on my post hospital care was taken and the whole matter was made even more comical by yet another patient in the ward, decidedly wobbly on his feet going on a walkabout whilst physio were trying to coax him back into a wheelchair. I relayed all this to Wendy and we both agreed that the story lay more in the auspices of a "Carry on" film. My spirit lifted. Wendy's chat with me enabled me to transcend worry. I was able to look beyond the worry of going into a nursing home. I was able to look beyond whether or not I should have had four (or was it five) sessions of radiotherapy and look instead at the noble ordinary person who God had sent to me.

This same Wendy now bought me a second get-well card and, by now, I knew the prognosis of my condition. I was so glad to see Wendy again, I shed a few tears. My second get-well card was from Louise.

"You know Louise," said Wendy.

I confessed I did not know Louise, yet she had also taken the trouble to write a card. She sounded like a lovely person who had reached out to me. My thoughts turned to whatever is lovely.

Male patients around me were aware of my faith yet with each conversation, each humorous moment shared, we grew closer as we met our various adversities. Jesus mixed with the poor and needy and Christian men should not be afraid of sharing with one another.

I wondered perhaps whether Paul might have believed himself to be in the Valley of the Shadow of Death when he wrote to the church at Philippi as he languished in prison, helpless, as I was seemingly helpless. Nevertheless, he wanted to emphasise that, in spite of everything, he was "... content whatever the circumstances" v11. Then he repeats the claim that he has "... learned the secret of being content in any and every situation" v12.

Could I, wrestling spiritually sore and bruised in a deep pit, claim the same? Could I say that I was content? I think we might all understand that my pit-bottom was not really a place of contentment. Yet things happened in that hospital as I slid and slithered to the Valley Floor. Things and people that told me that God was there, I was not abandoned. In fact, I was not alone at all. I began to piece it together.

Remembering the table

I started where I began – with worry. I remembered a simple truth; it is quite impossible to be content if we are worried. The problem is that we cannot just get rid of worry and I believe that all worriers would agree with me. This is the problem addressed by Paul. "Do not be anxious about anything" says Paul, instead he urges us to think on a list of god-characteristics – whatever is true, noble, just, lovely, admirable, excellent and praiseworthy which I have reflected on in the first ten chapters of the book. Effectively we are replacing worry with something else. However, we saw that the list also presents its own challenges to overcome. We recognise that each characteristic presents an aspect of God's character, which might be at odds with our character. Looking at the person or character of God might enable us to transcend or look beyond whatever worry besets us.

I then remembered a second, but not so simple, truth. Transcending worry does not necessarily produce contentment. Transcending worry is a big stepping-stone toward contentment but more has to be understood to unlock the "secret" of contentment. This is what I have tried to achieve in the last five chapters of the book.

As I start remembering the table, I humbly bought my shattered faith to Jesus who had died on the cross but had now risen from the tomb. I took hold of Jesus knowing that, in him, I could rise with him. With him, I could get off the floor. All Christians can confidently hold onto the prerogative that Jesus invites us to this table and, as this is a table of resurrection, we can be certain that we are going up. This is common to us all. From then on how we rise from the Valley in this life can vary enormously. Anyone who has been through this experience will have a different story to tell.

Remembering those supporting me in prayer

Family and friends are so important to us especially when going through the Shadow of the Valley of Death. It is a big added extension if they are praying as well. Throughout my long fall, I have been conscious of those who have been praying constantly for me over that time. "The Lord is near," writes Paul. I know he is near but I need constant reminding because it is only too easy to think that God has departed and gone away.

I have a close-knit group of family and friends who I knew were praying for me as well as my beautiful church but God chose David and Maureen, my brother/sister in law to do something in response to their prayers. They sent me some music or more particularly it was the words to the music but I really loved the song and the beat. It is called, "The battle belongs to you."

> *When all I see is the battle, you see my victory*
> *When all I see is a mountain, I see a mountain moved.*
> *And when I walked through the Shadow,*
> *your love surrounds me*
> *There's nothing to fear now, for I am safe with you.*
> *So when I fight, I fight on my knees*
> *with my hand lifted high.*
> *Oh God the battle belongs to you,*
> *every fear I lay at your feet.*
> *I'll sing through the night,*
> *Oh God the battle belongs to you.*
> *And if you are for me who can be against me?*
> *For Jesus there is nothing impossible for you.*
> *When all I see are the ashes, you see the beauty.*
> *When all I see is the cross, you see the empty tomb.*

When I first received this from David and Maureen, I could not see its relevance. My daily readings seemed, if anything, to be guiding down paths of rest, peace, and trust. I was not envisaging battle. Then I realised that, although there was a battle and it was raging around me, that battle was not mine to fight except through prayer to God, who would do the fighting. Negative thoughts were flying through my head as I lay in my hospital bed but now, when this happened, out came the phone, on went the earplugs and I played the tape. I needed to play it repeatedly. I believe God knew my need so provided for me.

Remembering a panoply of ordinary people

However, the aspect of support, which surprised me most, was the support I got from the ordinary people that I met. Yes, I had some expectation regarding the nursing staff but what I did not expect was the ability to share both faith and friendship with people I did not know. When I piece these together, it produces a panoply of sheer beauty.

Duncan was on the palliative care team. His bedside visits were frequent and on one such occasion, he was talking about life expectancy.

"Oh this is in my Bible reading for today," I said.

Duncan looked at me questioning and I took the opportunity to explain to him that I read a Bible passage each morning, which formed the basis of my prayers and meditation.

"This morning's reading was Matthew 6 which says, 'Do not worry about your life'.

Duncan's eyes widened. "Well you can't get better than that," he said.

Then there were visitors to other patients. One such lady, elderly and with a walking stick offered to give me a cuddle.

"Yes please," I replied. This is where humility steps in. We should not be afraid to accept offers like this when we need a cuddle and, right then, I needed one.

In the ward bed opposite, lay David. He had Parkinson's disease and was most intent on discharge. Every night he would fight the ward staff by trying to walk out. He also wanted, for some reason, to talk to me. One night, David managed to evade the staff radar and staggered uncertainly over toward me. The light were off and I was asleep. Suddenly I was aware of this ghostly apparition in a hospital gown appearing over my head. I nearly jumped out of bed even in my condition. Thankfully, the staff were not far away. The last night of David's hospital stay was more in keeping with twelve rounds with Mike Tyson where David fought all night for his release, I couldn't help but admire his tenacity yet felt much sympathy for the hospital staff endeavouring to look after him. He wore himself out so much that he slept through the next morning and never did get to see his homecoming. So human!

There was Hassan. He was a young doctor on the wards who came to see me about my problems. The hospital wanted to carry out a minor procedure but they kept putting it off. Four times, it was scheduled and then postponed. Eventually, in view of my oncology prognosis, we decided to shelve it. After the consultant departed my bedside, I noticed Hassan doing "grateful" arm movements.

"I am so grateful to you," he said, "and all you have taught me".

I looked at him. What had I taught him? Afterwards one of the nurses confirmed that he had been talking about how much he had learned from me. I will most likely never know but it does not matter. God inspired him somehow through me and that was wonderful to know.

Finally, carers are now looking after me at home. I think of one occasion when they could give me a bit of time and we talked about Richard. Two ordinary women helping me and yet sharing their own experiences and at the same time finding them very open to understanding that we are all in God's hand.

This small but dazzling display of caring people of differing race, faith and denomination were surrounding me as I struggled with feelings of isolation in my problems. People created in the image of God whose natural inclination is not to lean towards God. Even those who might say that they do not believe in God, swayed as many are by those who say that there is a God. These people are frustrated because they want to offer more care but are prevented from doing so through staff shortages, lack of time, or by layers of rules upon rules. Even in this "down in the pit" situation, I felt a surge of utter contentment as I remembered these ordinary people who surrounded me.

This is my experience of finding the "secret of being content in any and every situation". People, ordinary everyday people, some doing their job, some just other patients in the ward, but all coming alongside me. Jesus had led these people to me. I too had been led towards them. They served me in my time of need but most extraordinarily, I was able to serve them in spite of my complex physical problems and needs. It made me think whatever our circumstances, we can serve Jesus. This was my contentment; I was fulfilling my purpose in this place. I was serving Jesus even in these difficult circumstances. This led me up out of the mental and emotional pit. This was resurrection. Without Jesus, I had no hope. This required humility on my part, as there was no way up by my own efforts. He sent me a panoply of beautiful ordinary people to help me and I humbly accepted that help and support. As in the parable of the vineyard, I was in the market place ready and willing to be called to work for Him.

In this, I know that I am not alone. I am thinking of Paul and consider that perhaps he too went through much the same. At the end of the Acts of the Apostles, we read in the last verse v31, "(Paul) proclaimed the kingdom of God and taught about the Lord Jesus Christ – with all boldness and without hindrance". Contentment! Paul in Rome held for trial soon to be martyred, was content. He was serving the Lord whether he was waiting in the market place or working in the vineyard.

Does this mean that to find contentment we have to go through what I went through? Certainly not! As God leads us, we can each find contentment in any and every situation at any stage of our life. I must finish with what I have constantly emphasised that this is my story of transcending worry and finding contentment. You will have a different story to tell about your journey.

Paul winds it up with a masterful shout of triumph. "I can do all things through him who gives me strength," Philippians 4:13. All things may be different things. Our experience of finding the secret of being content in any and every situation will undoubtedly differ. My secret lay in service and although I now have no bodily strength, God allowed me to share my faith with others and in turn to humbly accept their support for me. I will remember them for the rest of the life given to me, as I believe they will remember me.

Where from here? Like everybody else, I do not know. None of us knows what God has in store for us. I see myself as many do, as part of Psalm 23 which I have alluded to many times in this book. I see myself seated around a table with Jesus in the presence of my enemies, worry being the foremost. I see myself at times with my faith in tatters humbly dependant on Jesus yet in the market place, ready to be called into the vineyard. I have reached the bottom and realise that I am not alone. The Lord is near. I am now emerging but to what? Sally and I are fortunate enough to live by still waters. Perhaps God might allow me to live out my life beside this pasture for a while. One thing we both know for a certainty. "We shall dwell in the house of the Lord – forever."

EPILOGUE

John was home from hospital for 10 days. It was a very precious time and one where we experienced joy and contentment, how was that humanly possible? Sadly, he died on 19 October 2022. He was working on this book right up until he went into hospital at midday on 18 October. He realised that whilst he was writing the last chapter of this book, he was also writing the last chapter in his life.

He worked on this book for well over two years, re-writing, refining and making alterations. He very much believed God called him to write. He wanted to share this with others through publication.

It took me some months after John died for me to have the courage to look at the book, particularly the final chapter, and see what was required. Courage because of the responsibility I felt towards getting it in good shape and fear of letting myself in for even more pain than I was already experiencing. However, reading it did not have that affect. I found myself very much in tune with John; I had a purpose and a job to complete and was able, with the help of God, to do the necessary. After all, this book has been part of my life for so long, reading all the re-writes! In fact, I remember saying to John, "don't you die before you finish it, I do not want the responsibility". He kept a journal whilst in hospital. Throughout he writes this prayer, *"Lord please let me live long enough to finish the book"*. His prayer and the prayers of all the people who loved him, I see answered on that score.

His final entry in his journal was on 15 October he wrote:

"What do I make of Jeremiah 29, in my circumstances (verse 11), "I have plans for you…?" Surely, it looks like plans for dying and rising with Jesus. Yet here I have a reading that is about me continuing to live on earth. It raises the question. Where are we going Lord? I am preparing to die yet I do not feel ready to die. I have 10 years in me.

However, is God saying, "No you are coming to me."

What is to be? I do not know so I cannot pray. I am leaving that to others.

One thing or another right now, I am in captivity. My body has shut down. If I am to be released it is either through death or a miracle. It all looks like death but Lord, have you anything else in mind?

Yours waiting in the market place.

John"

My prayer is that I hope this book speaks to you in some way, because that was the desire of John's heart, to serve God, and let Him do the rest.

Sally Bloor

February 2023